Y0-CLX-610

Mrs. Wiggs
of the Cabbage Patch

By
ALICE
HEGAN
RICE

Illustrated by
Norma and Dan Garris

WHITMAN PUBLISHING COMPANY
Racine, Wisconsin

Copyright © 1962, by
WHITMAN PUBLISHING COMPANY
PRINTED IN U.S.A.

Contents

1. Mrs. Wiggs's Philosophy 9
2. Ways and Means 20
3. The "Christmas Lady" 33
4. The Annexation of Cuby 45
5. A Reminiscence 53
6. A Theater Party 63
7. "Mr. Bob" 78
8. Mrs. Wiggs At Home 90
9. How Spring Came to the Cabbage Patch 103
10. Australia's Mishap 116
11. The Benefit Dance 126

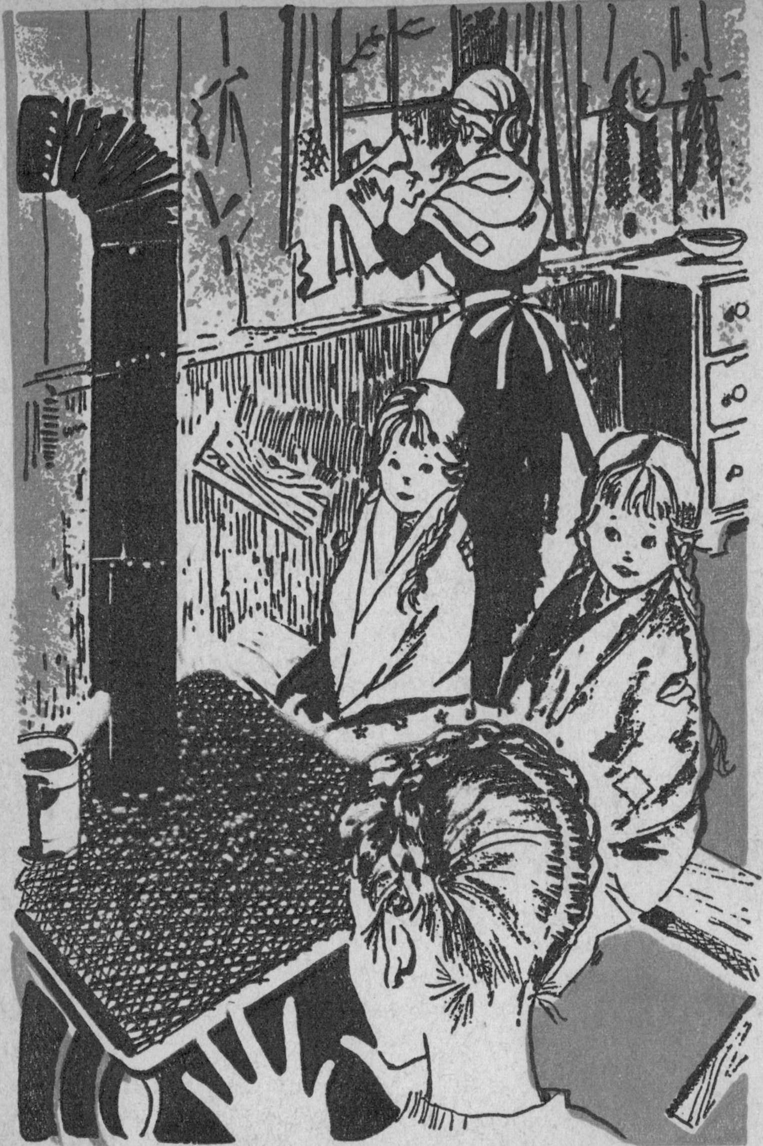

1

Mrs. Wiggs's Philosophy

"In the mud and scum of things
Something always, always sings!"

"My, but it's nice an' cold this mornin'! The thermometer's done fell up to zero!"

Mrs. Wiggs made the statement as cheerfully as if her elbows were not sticking out through the boy's coat that she wore, or her teeth chattering in her head like a pair of castanets. But, then, Mrs. Wiggs was a philosopher, and the sum and substance of her philosophy lay in keeping the dust off her rose-colored spectacles. When Mr. Wiggs traveled to eternity by the alcohol route, she buried his faults with him, and for want of better virtues to extol she always laid stress on the fine hand he wrote. It was the same way when their little country home burned and she had to come to the city to seek work; her one comment was: "Thank God, it was the pig instid of the baby that was burned!"

So this bleak morning in December she pinned the bedclothes around the children and made them sit up close to the stove, while she pasted brown paper over the broken windowpane and made sprightly comments on the change in the weather.

The Wiggses lived in the Cabbage Patch. It was not a real cabbage patch, but a strange neighborhood, where ramshackle cottages played hopscotch over the railroad tracks. There were no streets, so when a new house was built the owner faced it any way his fancy prompted. Mr. Bagby's grocery, it is true, conformed to convention, and presented a solid front to the railroad track. But Miss Hazy's cottage shied off sidewise into the Wiggses' yard, as if it were afraid of the big freight trains that went thundering past so many times a day, and Mrs. Schultz's front room looked directly into the Eichorns' kitchen. The latter was not a bad arrangement, however, for Mrs. Schultz had been confined to her bed for ten years, and her sole interest in life consisted in watching what took place in her neighbor's family.

The Wiggses' house was the most imposing in the neighborhood. This was probably due to the fact that it had two front doors and a tin roof. One door was nailed up, and the other opened outdoors, but you would never guess it from the street. When the country house burned, one door had been saved. So Mrs. Wiggs and the boys brought it to the new home and skillfully placed it at the front end of the side porch. But the roof gave the house its chief distinction; it was the only tin roof in the Cabbage Patch. Jim and Billy had made it of old cans which they picked up on the commons.

Jim was fifteen and head of the family; his shoulders were those of a man, and were bent with work, but his body dwindled away to a pair of thin legs that seemed incapable of supporting the burden imposed upon them. In his anxious eyes was the look of a breadwinner who had begun the struggle too soon. Life had been a tragedy to Jim: the tragedy that comes when a child's sensitive soul is forced to meet the responsibilities of manhood, yet lacks the wisdom that only experience can bring.

Billy Wiggs was differently constituted; responsibilities rested upon him as lightly as the freckles on his nose. When occasion or his mother demanded he worked to good purpose, with a tenacity that argued well for his future success, but for the most part he played and fought and got into trouble with the aptitude characteristic of the average small boy.

It was Mrs. Wiggs's boast that her three little girls had geography names; first came Asia, then Australia. When the last baby arrived, Billy had stood looking down at the small bundle and asked anxiously, "Are you goin' to have it fer a boy or a girl, Ma?" Mrs. Wiggs had answered, "A girl, Billy, an' her name's Europena!"

On this particular Sunday morning Mrs. Wiggs

bustled about the kitchen in unusual haste.

"I am goin' to make you all some nice Irish pertater soup fer dinner," she said, as she came in from the parlor, where she kept her potatoes and onions. "The boys'll be in soon, an' we'll have to hurry and git through 'fore the childern begin comin' to Sunday school."

For many years Sunday afternoon had been a trying time in the neighborhood, so Mrs. Wiggs had organized a Sunday school class at which she presided.

"If there don't come Chris an' Pete a'ready!" said Asia, from her post by the stove. "I bet they've had their dinner an' jes' come early to git some of ours!"

"Why, Asia!" exclaimed Mrs. Wiggs. "That ain't hospit'le, an' Chris with one leg, too! 'Tain't no trouble at all. All I got to do is to put a little more water in the soup, an' me and Jim won't take but one piece of bread."

When Jim and Billy came in they found their places at the table taken, so they sat on the floor and drank their soup out of teacups.

"Gee!" said Billy, after the third helping, "I've drinken so much that when I swallers a piece er bread I can hear it splash!"

"Well, you boys git up now, an' go out and bring me in a couple of planks to put acrost the cheers fer the childern to set on."

By two o'clock the Sunday school had begun. Every seat in the kitchen, available and otherwise, was occupied. The boys sat in the windows and on the table, and the girls squeezed together on the improvised benches. Mrs. Wiggs stood before them with a dilapidated hymnbook in her hand.

"Now, you all must hush talkin', so we kin all sing a hymn. I'll read it over, then we'll all sing it together.

>'When upon life's billers you are
>   tempest tossed,
>When you are discouraged thinkin'
>   all is lost,
>Count yer many blessin's, name 'em
>   one by one,
>An' it will surprise you what the Lord
>   hath done!'"

Clear and strong rose the childish voices in different keys and regardless of time, but with a genuine enthusiasm that was in itself a blessing. When they had sung through three stanzas Mrs. Wiggs began the lesson.

"What did we study 'bout last Sunday?" she asked.

No response, save a smothered giggle from two of the little girls.

"Don't you all remember what the Lord give Moses up on the mountain?"

A hand went up in the corner, and an eager voice cried, "Yas'm, I know! Lord give Moses ten tallers, an' he duveled 'em."

Before Mrs. Wiggs could enter into an argument concerning this new version of sacred history, she was hit in the eye with a paper wad. It was aimed at Billy, but when he dodged she became the victim. This caused some delay, for she had to bathe the injured member, and during the interval the Sunday school became riotous.

"Mith Wiggs, make Tommy thop thpittin' terbaccer juice in my hat!"

"Miss Wiggs, I know who hit you!"

"Teacher, kin I git a drink?"

It was not until Mrs. Wiggs, with a stocking tied over her eye, emerged from the bedroom and again took command that order was restored.

"Where is Bethlehem?" she began, reading from an old lesson paper.

"You kin search *me!*" promptly answered Chris.

She ignored his remark, and passed to the next, who said, half doubtfully, "Ain't it in Alabama?"

"No, it's in the Holy Land," she said.

A sudden commotion arose in the back of the room. Billy, by a series of skillful maneuvers, had succeeded in removing the chair that held one of the planks, and a cascade of small, indignant girls were tobogganing sidewise down the incline. A fight was imminent, but before any further trouble occurred Mrs. Wiggs locked Billy in the bedroom and became mistress of the situation.

"What I think you childern need is a talk about fussin' an' fightin'. There ain't no use in me teachin' what they done a thousand years ago, when you ain't got manners 'nough to listen at what I am sayin'. I recollect one time durin' the war, when the soldiers was layin' 'round the camp, tryin' they best to keep from freezin' to death, a preacher come 'long to hold a service. An' when he got up to preach he sez, 'Friends,' sez he, 'my tex' is Chilblains. They ain't no use a-preachin' religion to men whose whole thought is set on their feet. Now, you fellows git some soft soap an' pour it in yer shoes, an' jes' keep them shoes on till yer feet gits well, an' the nex' time I come 'round yer minds'll be better prepared to receive the word of the Lord.' Now, that's the way I feel 'bout this here Sunday school. First an' fo'most, I am goin' to learn you all manners. Jes' one thought I want you to take away, an' that is, it's sinful to fuss. Ma use' to say livin' was like quiltin' —you orter keep the peace an' do 'way with the scraps. Now, what do I want you to remember?"

"Don't fuss!" came the prompt answer.

"That's right. Now we'll all sing 'Pull fer the Shore.'"

When the windows had ceased to rattle from the vibrations of the lusty chorus, Mrs. Wiggs lifted her hands for silence.

"O Lord!" she prayed earnestly, "help these here childern to be good an' kind to each other, an' to their mas an' their pas. Make 'em thankful fer whatever they've got, even if it ain't but a little. Show us all how to live like you want us to live, an' praise God from whom all blessin's flow. Amen."

As the last youngster scampered out of the yard, Mrs. Wiggs turned to the window where Jim was standing. He had taken no part in the singing and was silent and preoccupied. "Jim," said his mother, trying to look into his face, "you never had on yer overcoat when you come in. You ain't gone an' sold it?"

"Yes," said the boy heavily. "But 'tain't 'nough fer the rent. I got to figger it out some other way."

Mrs. Wiggs put her arm about his shoulder, and together they looked out across the dreary commons.

"Don't you worry so, Jimmy," said she. "Mebbe I kin git work tomorraw, or you'll git a raise, or somethin'. They'll be some way."

Little she guessed what the way was to be.

2

Ways and Means

"Ah! well may the children weep before you!
  They are weary ere they run;
They have never seen the sunshine, nor the glory
  Which is brighter than the sun."

The cold wave that was ushered in that December morning was the beginning of a long series of days that vied with each other as to which could induce the mercury to drop the lowest. The descent of the temperature seemed to have a like effect on the barrel of potatoes and the load of coal in the Wiggses' parlor.

Mrs. Wiggs's untiring efforts to find employment had met with no success, and Jim's exertions were redoubled. Day by day his scanty earnings became less sufficient to meet the demands of the hungry family.

On Christmas Eve they sat near the stove, after the little ones had gone to bed, and discussed the situation. The wind hurled itself against the house in a very frenzy of rage, shaking the icicles from the window ledge and hissing through the patched panes. The snow that sifted in through the loose sash lay unmelted on the sill. Jim had a piece of old carpet about him and coughed with almost every breath. Mrs. Wiggs's head was in her hands, and the tears that trickled through her crooked fingers hissed as they fell on the stove. It was the first time Jim had ever seen her give up.

"Seems like we'll have to ast fer help, Jim," she said. "I can't ast fer credit at Mr. Bagby's; seems like I'd never have the courage to pull agin a debt. What do you think? I guess it looks like mebbe we'll have to apply to the organization."

Jim's eyes flashed. "Not yet, Ma!" he said firmly. "It 'ud be with us like it was with the Hornbys. They didn't have nothin' to eat, and they went to the organization an' the man asted 'em if they had a bed or a table, an' when they said yes, he said, 'Well, why don't you sell 'em?'

No, Ma! As long as we've got coal I'll git the vittles some way!" He had to pause, for a violent attack of coughing shook him from head to foot. "I think I can git a night job next week; one of the market men comes in from the country ever' night to git a early start nex' mornin', an' he ast me if I'd sleep in his wagon from three to six an' keep his vegetables from bein' stole. That 'ud gimme time to git home an' git breakfast, an' be down to the fact'ry by seven."

"But, Jimmy boy," cried his mother, her voice quivering with anxiety, "you never could stan' it night an' day, too! No, I'll watch the wagon. I'll—"

A knock on the parlor door interrupted her. She hastily dried her eyes and smoothed her hair. Jim went to the door.

"I've a Christmas basket for you!" cried a cheery voice.

"Is this Christmas?" Jim asked dully.

The girl in the doorway laughed. She was tall and slender, but Jim could only see a pair of sparkling eyes between the brim of the hat and

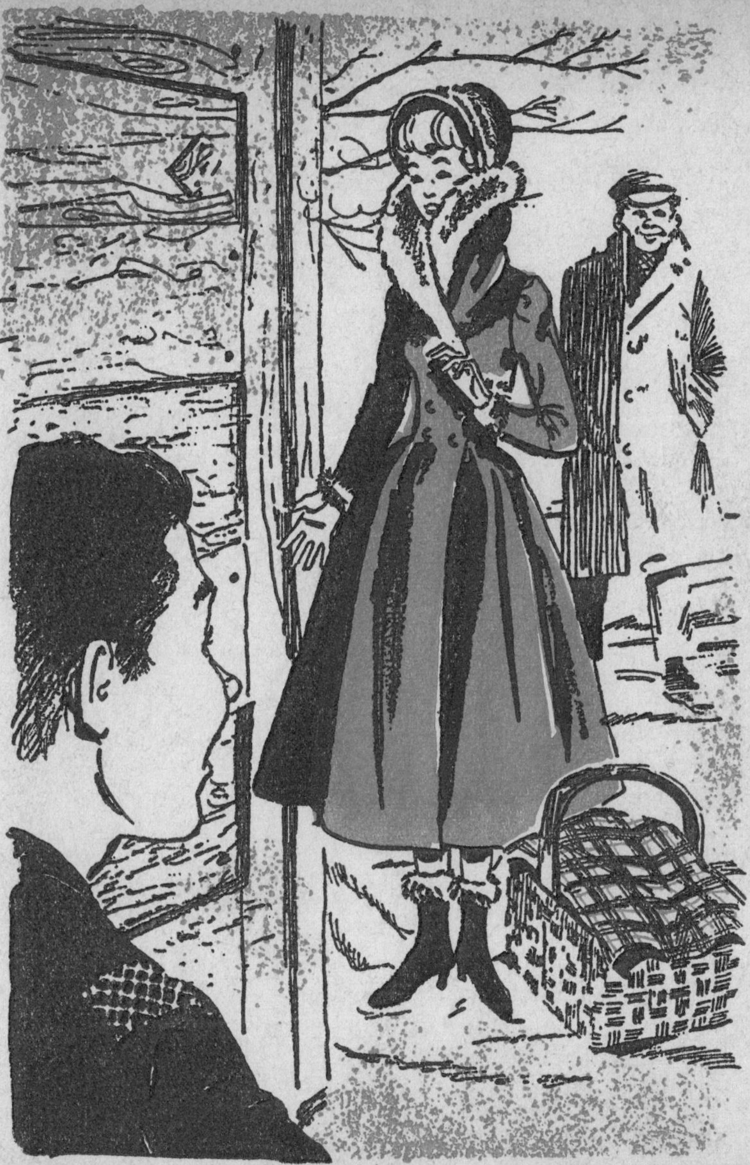

her high fur collar. It was nice to hear her laugh, though. It made things seem warmer somehow. The colored man behind her deposited a large basket on the doorstep.

"It's from the church," she explained. "A crowd of us are out in the bus distributing baskets."

"Well, how'd you ever happen to come here?" cried Mrs. Wiggs, who had come to the door.

"There is one for each of the mission school families; just a little Christmas greeting, you know."

Mrs. Wiggs's spirits were rising every minute. "That certainly is kind an' thoughtful like," she said. "Won't you—" then she hesitated. The room she had just left was not in a condition to receive guests, but Mrs. Wiggs was a Kentuckian. "Come right in an' git warm," she said cordially. "The stove's died down some, but you could git thawed out."

"No, thank you, I can't come in," said the young lady with a side glance at Jim who was leaning against the door. "Have you plenty of coal?" she asked in an undertone.

"Oh, yes'm, thank you," said Mrs. Wiggs, smiling reassuringly. Her tone might have been less confident but for Jim's warning glance. Every fiber of his sensitive nature shrank from asking help.

The girl was puzzled. She noticed the stamp of poverty on everything in sight except the bright face of the little woman before her.

"Well," she said doubtfully, "if you ever want —to come to see me, ask for Miss Lucy Olcott at Terrace Park. Good night, and a happy Christmas!"

She was gone, and the doorway looked very black and lonesome in consequence. But there was the big basket to prove she was not merely an apparition, and it took both Jim and his mother to carry it into the house. Sitting on the floor, they unpacked it. There were vegetables, oatmeal, fruit, and even tea and coffee. But the surprise was at the very bottom! A big turkey, looking so comical with his legs stuck in his body that Jim laughed outright.

"It's the first turkey that's been in this house

fer many a day!" said Mrs. Wiggs delightedly, as she pinched the fat fowl. "I 'spect Europena'll be skeered of it, it's so big. My, but we'll have a good dinner tomorra! I'll git Miss Hazy an' Chris to come over an' spend the day, an' I'll carry a plate over to Mrs. Schultz an' take a little o' this here tea to ole Mrs. Lawson."

The cloud had turned inside out for Mrs. Wiggs, and only the silver lining was visible. Jim was doing a sum on the brown paper that came over the basket, and presently he looked up and said slowly, "Ma, I guess we can't have the turkey this year. I kin sell it fer a dollar seventy-five, and that would buy us hog meat fer a good while."

Mrs. Wiggs's face fell, and she twisted her apron string in silence. She had pictured the joy of a real Christmas dinner, the first the youngest children had ever known. And she had already thought of half a dozen neighbors to whom she wanted to send "a little snack." But one look at Jim's anxious face recalled their circumstances.

"Of course we'll sell it," she said brightly. "You have got the longest head fer a boy! We'll sell it in the mornin' an' buy sausage fer dinner, an' I'll cook some of these here nice vegetables an' put a orange an' some candy at each plate, an' the childern'll never know nothin' 'bout it. Besides," she added, "if you ain't never et turkey meat you don't know how good it is."

But in spite of her philosophy, after Jim had gone to bed she slipped over and took one more look at the turkey.

"I think I wouldn't 'a' minded so much," she said wistfully, "ef they hadn't sent the cramberries, too!"

For ten days the basket of provisions and the extra money made by Jim's night work and Mrs. Wiggs's washing supplied the demands of the family. But by the end of January the clouds had gathered thicker than before.

Mrs. Wiggs's heart was heavy one night as she tramped home through the snow after a hard day's work. The rent was due, the coal was out, and only a few potatoes were left in the barrel. But these were mere shadow troubles, compared to Jim's illness. He had been too sick to go to the factory that morning, and she dared not think what changes the day may have brought. As she lifted the latch of her rickety door the sobbing of a child greeted her; it was little Europena, crying for food. For three days there had been no bread in the house, and a scanty supply of potatoes and beans had been their only nourishment.

Mrs. Wiggs hastened to where Jim lay on a cot in the corner. His cheeks were flushed and his thin, nervous fingers picked at the old shawl that covered him.

"Jim," she said, kneeling beside him and pressing his hot hand to her cheek, "Jim, darlin', lemme go fer the doctor. You're worser than you was this mornin', an'—an'—I'm so skeered!" Her voice broke in a sob.

Jim tried to put his arm around her but something hurt him in his chest when he moved, so he patted her hand instead.

"Never mind, Ma," he said, his breath coming short. "We ain't got no money to buy the medicine, even if the doctor did come. You go git some supper, now. An', Ma, don't worry. I'm goin' to take keer of you all! Only—only," he added wearily, "I guess I can't sleep in the wagon tonight."

Slowly the hours passed until midnight. Mrs. Wiggs had pulled Jim's cot close to the stove, and applied vigorous measures to relieve him. Her efforts were unceasing, and one after another the homely country remedies were faithfully administered. At twelve o'clock he grew restless.

"Seems like I'm hot, then agin I'm cold," he said, speaking with difficulty. "Could you find a little somethin' more to put over me, Ma?"

Mrs. Wiggs got up and went toward the bed. The three little girls lay huddled under one old quilt, their faces pale and sunken. She turned away abruptly and looked toward the corner where Billy slept on a pallet. The blankets on his bed were insufficient even for him. She put her hands over her face, and for a moment dry sobs convulsed her. The hardest grief is often that which leaves no trace. When she went back to the stove she had a smile ready for the sick boy.

"Here's the very thing," she said. "It's my dress skirt. I don't need it a mite, settin' up here so clost to the fire. See how nice it tucks in all 'round!"

For a while he lay silent, then he said, "Ma, are you 'wake?"

"Yes, Jim."

"Well, I bin thinkin' it over. If I ain't better in the mornin', I guess—" the words came reluctantly, "I guess you'd better go see the Christmas lady. I wouldn't mind her knowin' so much. 'Twon't be fer long, nohow, cause I kin take keer of you all soon—soon's I kin git up."

The talking brought on severe coughing, and he sank back exhausted.

"Can't you go to sleep, honey?" asked his mother.

"No, it's them ole wheels," he said fretfully, "them wheels at the fact'ry. When I git to sleep they keep on wakin' me up."

Mrs. Wiggs's hands were rough and knotted, but love taught them to be gentle as she smoothed his hot head.

"Want me to tell you 'bout the country, Jim?"

Since he was a little boy he had loved to hear of their old home in the valley. His dim recollection of it all formed his one conception of heaven.

"Yes, Ma. Mebbe it will make me fergit the wheels," he said.

"Well," she began, putting her head beside his on the pillow, so he could not watch her face, "it was all jes' like a big front yard without no fences. An' the flowers didn't belong to folks like they do over on the avenue, where you dassent pick a one. They was God's, an' you was welcome to all you could pull. An' there was trees where you could climb up an' git big red apples, Jim. An' when the frost 'ud come they'd be persimmons that 'ud jes' melt in yer mouth. An' you could look 'way off 'crost the meaders an' see the trees a wavin' in the sunshine, an' up over yer head the birds 'ud be singin' like they was never goin' to stop. An' yer pa an' me 'ud take you out at the harvestin' time, an' you 'ud play on the haystacks. I kin remember jes' how you looked, Jim—a fat little boy, with red cheeks, a-laughin' all the time."

Mrs. Wiggs could tell no more, for the old

memories were too much for her. Jim scarcely knew when she stopped. His eyes were half closed and a sweet drowsiness was upon him.

"It's nice an' warm in the sunshine," he murmured. "The meaders an' trees—laughin' all the time! Birds singin', singin', singin'."

Then Jim began to sing, too, softly and monotonously, and the sorrow that had not come with years left his tired face, and he fearlessly drifted away into the Shadowy Valley where his lost childhood lay.

3

The "Christmas Lady"

"The rosy glow of summer
  Is on thy dimpled cheek,
While in thy heart the winter
  Is lying cold and bleak.

"But this shall change hereafter,
  When years have done their part,
And on thy cheek the winter,
  And summer in thy heart."

Late the next afternoon a man and a girl were standing in the Olcott reception hall. The lamps had not been lighted but the blaze from the backlog threw a cozy glow of comfort over the crimson curtains and on the mass of bright-hued pillows in the window seat.

Robert Redding, standing with his hat in his hand, would have been gone long ago if the "Christmas Lady" had not worn her violet gown. He said it always took him half an hour to say good-by when she wore a rose in her hair, and a full hour when she had on the violet dress.

"By Jove, stand there a minute just as you are! The firelight shining through your hair makes you look like a saint. Little Saint Lucinda!" he said teasingly, as he tried to catch her hand. She put it behind her for safekeeping.

"Not a saint at all?" he went on, in mock surprise. "Then an iceberg—a nice, proper little iceberg."

Lucy Olcott looked up at him for a moment, in silence. He was very tall and straight, and his face retained much of its boyishness, in spite of the firm, square jaw.

"Robert," she said, suddenly grown serious, "I wish you would do something for me."

"All right, what is it?" he asked.

She timidly put her hand on his and looked up at him earnestly.

"It's about Dick Harris," she said. "I wish you would not be with him so much."

Redding's face clouded. "You aren't afraid to trust me?" he asked.

"Oh, no! It isn't that," she said hurriedly. "But, Robert, it makes people think such wrong things about you. I can't bear to have you misjudged."

Redding put his arm around her and together they stood looking down into the glowing embers.

"Tell me about it, little girl. What have you heard?" he asked.

She hesitated. "It wasn't true what they said. I knew it wasn't true, but they had no right to say it."

"Well, let's hear it, anyway. What was it?"

"Some people were here last night from New Orleans and they asked if I knew you—said they knew you and Dick the year you spent there."

"Well?" said Redding.

Lucy evidently found it difficult to continue. "They said some horrid things then, just because you were Dick's friend."

"What were they, Lucy?"

"They told me that you were both as wild as could be; that your reputation was no better than his; that—forgive me, Robert, for even repeating it. It made me very angry, and I told them it was not true—not a word of it; that it was all Dick's fault; that he—"

"Lucy," interrupted Redding peremptorily, "wait until you hear me! I have never lied to you about anything, and I will not stoop to it now. Four years ago, when those people knew me, I was just what they said. Dick Harris and I went to New Orleans straight from college. Neither of us had a home or people to care about us, so we went in for a good time. At the end of the year I was sick of it all, braced up, and came here. Poor Dick, he kept on."

At his first words the color had left Lucy's face, and she had slipped to the opposite side of the fire. She stood watching him with horrified eyes.

"But you were never like Dick!" she protested.

"Yes," he continued passionately, "and but for God's help I should be like him still. It was an awful pull, and Heaven only knows how I struggled. I never quite saw the use of it all, until I met you six months ago; then I realized that the past four years had been given me in which to make a man of myself."

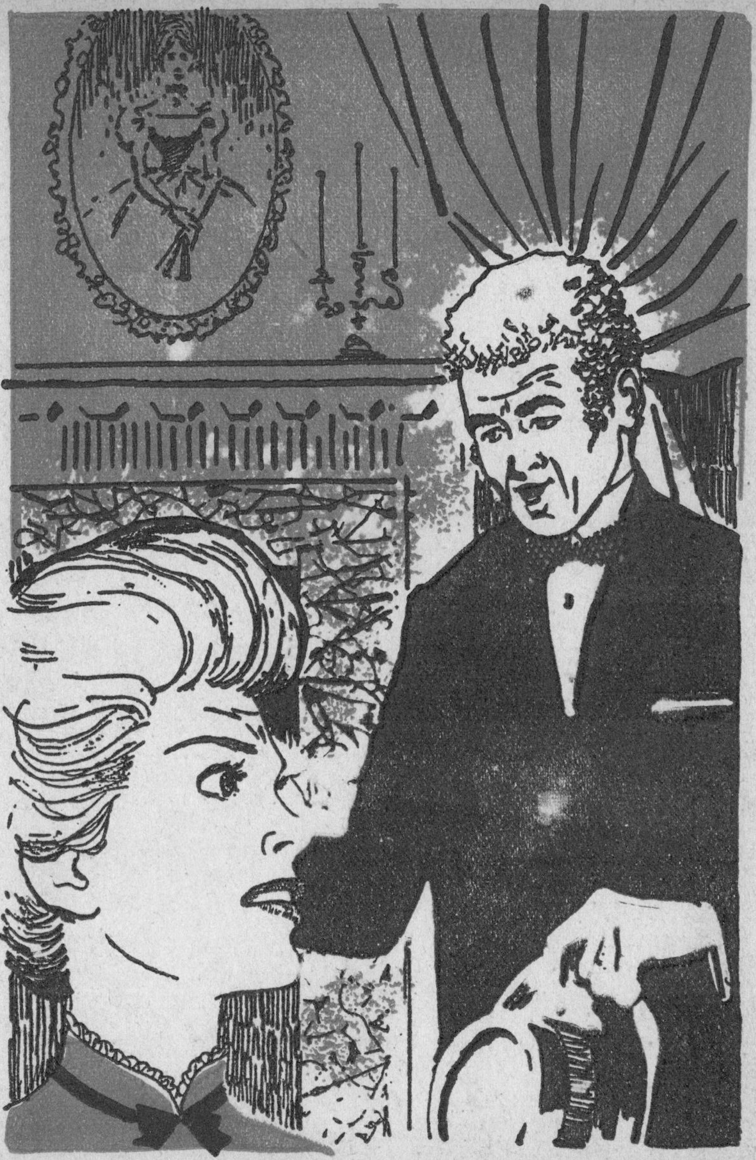

As he finished speaking he saw, for the first time, that Lucy was crying. He sprang forward but she shrank away. "No, no, don't touch me! I'm so terribly disappointed, and hurt, and—stunned."

"But you surely don't love me the less for having conquered these things in the past?"

"I don't know, I don't know," she said with a sob. "I honored and idealized you, Robert. I can never think of you as being other than you are now."

"But why should you?" he pleaded. "It was only one year out of my life. Too much, it's true, but I have atoned for it with all my might."

The intensity and earnestness of his voice were beginning to influence her. She was very young, with the stern, uncompromising standards of girlhood. Life was black or white to her, and time had not filled in the canvas with the myriad grays that blend into one another until all lines are effaced and only the Master Artist knows the boundaries.

She looked up through her tears. "I'll try to

forgive you," she said tremulously. "But you must promise to give up your friendship for Dick Harris."

Redding frowned and bit his lip. "That's not fair!" he said. "You know Dick's my chum; that he hasn't the least influence over me; that I am about the only one to stand by him."

"I am not afraid of his influence but I don't want people to see you together. It makes them say things."

"But, Lucy, you wouldn't have me go back on him? Dick has a big heart and he's trying to brace up—"

"Oh, nonsense!" cried Lucy impatiently. The fire in her eyes had dried the tears. "He could straighten up if he wanted to. He likes to drink and gamble, so he does it. You only encourage him by your friendship. Are you choosing between us?" she demanded angrily.

Redding's face was clouded and he spoke slowly. "You wouldn't ask this of me, Lucy, if you understood. Dick and I have been chums since we were boys. He came to Kentucky three months ago, sick and miserable. One day he came into the office and said, 'Bob, you've pulled through all right. Do you think it's too late for me to try?' What would you have said?"

"What you did, probably," answered Lucy, "but I would have profited by the one experience, for he has hardly drawn a sober breath since." She looked out of the window across the snowy landscape, and in her face was something of the passionless purity of the scene upon which her eyes rested.

"You are mistaken," he cried fiercely. "Because you have seen him several times in that condition, you have no right to draw such a conclusion. He is weak, nobody denies it; but what can you know of the struggle he makes, of his eagerness to do better, of the fight that he is constantly making with himself?"

His words fell on deaf ears.

"Then you choose Mr. Harris?"

"Lucy, this is madness! It is not like you in the least!"

The girl was cold with anger and excitement.

"It is bad enough," she said, "to know that my defense of you last night was worse than useless, but to have you persist in a friendship with a man who is beneath you in every way is more than I can stand." She slipped a ring from her finger and held it toward him. "I could never marry a man of whom I was ashamed."

The shot went home. There was a white line about Redding's mouth as he turned away.

"I would not ask you to," he said, with simple dignity, as he opened the door.

"Please, ma'am, is this Miss Olcott's?" asked a trembling voice on the piazza. A shabby woman stood looking at them with wild eyes. Her gray hair had escaped from the torn shawl that was pinned over her head, and stray locks blew across her face.

Lucy did not recognize her. "I will speak to you in a moment," she said.

An awkward pause followed, each waiting for the other to speak.

"I will come when you send for me," said Redding without looking at her and, turning abruptly, he strode down the steps and out into the dusk.

Lucy caught her breath and started forward; then she remembered the woman.

"What is it?" she asked listlessly.

The woman stepped forward and put out a hand to steady herself against the door. Her face was distorted and her voice came in gasps.

"You said I was to come if I needed you. It's Jimmy, ma'am—he's dead!"

It may be experience of suffering makes one especially tender to the heartaches of others; at any rate, the article that Lucy Olcott wrote for the paper that night held the one touch of nature that makes the whole world kin. She had taken Aunt Chloe, the old colored servant, and gone home with Mrs. Wiggs, relieving as far as possible the immediate needs of the family. Then she had come home and written their story, telling it simply, but with the passionate earnestness of one who, for the first time, has come into contact with poverty and starvation. She told of the plucky struggle made by the boy; of his indomitable courage; of his final defeat. She ended by asking help of any kind for the destitute family.

A week later she sat at her desk bewildered. Her article, written on the impulse of the moment, with the one thought of making people understand, had fulfilled its mission. For seven days she had done nothing but answer questions and notes and receive contributions for the Wiggs family. Money had arrived from all over the state and from every class of society. Eichenstine Brothers sent fifty dollars, and six ragged newsboys came to present thirty cents. A lavender note, with huge monogram and written in white ink, stated that some of the girls of the "Gay Burlesque Troupe" sent a few dimes to the "kid's" mother. The few dimes amounted to fifteen dollars. Mrs. Van Larkin's coachman had to wait with her note while Lucy answered the questions of a lame old Negro who had brought a quarter.

"Maria done tole me what was writ in de papah 'bout dat pore chile," he was saying. "I sutenly do feel sorry for his maw. I ain't got much, but

I jus' tole Maria I guess we could do without somethin' to gib a quahter."

So it continued. Old and young, rich and poor, paid their substantial tribute of respect to Jimmy Wiggs.

Lucy counted up the long line of figures. "Three hundred and sixty-five dollars!" she exclaimed. "And food, clothes, and coal enough to last them a year!"

It was like a direct answer to her prayer, and yet this poor little suppliant, instead of being duly exalted, put her head on the desk and wept bitterly. Now that the need of the Wiggs family had been met, another appeal, silent and potent, was troubling her heart.

Redding had neither come nor written, and she was beginning to realize the seriousness of their misunderstanding.

4

The Annexation of Cuby

"They well deserve to have,
That know the strongest and surest way to get."

Almost a year rolled over the Cabbage Patch and it was nearing Christmas again. The void left in Mrs. Wiggs's heart by Jim's death could never be filled, but time was beginning to soften her grief, and the necessity for steady employment kept her from brooding over her trouble.

It was still necessary to maintain the strictest economy, for half the money which had been given them was in Miss Olcott's keeping as a safeguard against another rainy day. Mrs. Wiggs had gotten as much washing as she could do; Asia helped about the house, and Billy did odd jobs wherever he could find them.

The direct road to fortune, however, according to Billy's ideas, could best be traveled in a kindling wagon, and, while he was the proud possessor of a dilapidated wagon, sole relic of the late Mr. Wiggs, he had nothing to hitch to it. Scarcely a week passed that he did not agitate the question, and, as Mrs. Wiggs often said, "When Billy Wiggs done set his head to a thing, he's as good as got it!"

So she was not surprised when he rushed breathlessly into the kitchen one evening about suppertime and exclaimed in excited tones, "Ma, I've got a horse! He was havin' a fit on the commons an' they was goin' to shoot him, an' I ast the man to give him to me!"

"My land, Billy! What do you want with a fit-horse?" asked his mother.

" 'Cause I knowed you could cure him. The man said if I took him I'd have to pay fer cartin' away his carcass, but I said, 'All right, I'll take him, anyway.' Come on, Ma, an' see him!" and Billy hurried back to his new possession.

Mrs. Wiggs pinned a shawl over her head and

ran across the commons. A group of men stood around the writhing animal, but the late owner had departed.

"He's 'most gone," said one of the men, as she came up. "I tole Billy you'd beat him fer takin' that ole nag offen the man's han's."

"Well, I won't," said Mrs. Wiggs stoutly. "Billy Wiggs's got more sense than most men I know. That hoss's carcass is worth somethin'. I 'spect he'd bring 'bout two dollars dead, an' mebbe more livin'. Anyway, I'm goin' to save him if there's any save to him!"

She stood with her arms on her hips and critically surveyed her patient. "I'll tell you what's the matter with him," was her final diagnosis. "His lights is riz. Billy, I'm goin' home fer some medicine. You set on his head so's he can't git up, an' Ma'll be right back in a minute."

The crowd which had collected to see the horse shot began to disperse, for it was suppertime, and there was nothing to see now but the poor suffering animal, with Billy Wiggs patiently sitting on its head.

When Mrs. Wiggs returned she carried a bottle and what appeared to be a large marble. "This here is a calomel pill," she explained. "I jes' rolled the calomel in with some soft, light bread. Now, you prop his jaw open with a little stick an' I'll shove it in. An' then hole his head back while I pour down some water an' turkentine outen this bottle."

It was with great difficulty that this was accomplished, for the old horse had evidently seen a vision of the happy hunting ground, and was loath to return to the sordid earth. His limbs were already stiffening in death and only the whites of his eyes were visible. Mrs. Wiggs noted these discouraging symptoms and saw that violent measures were necessary.

"Gether some sticks an' build a fire quick as you kin. I've got to run over home. Build it right clost to him, Billy. We've got to git him het up."

She rushed into the kitchen, and, taking several cakes of tallow from the shelf, threw them into a tin bucket. Then she hesitated for a moment. The

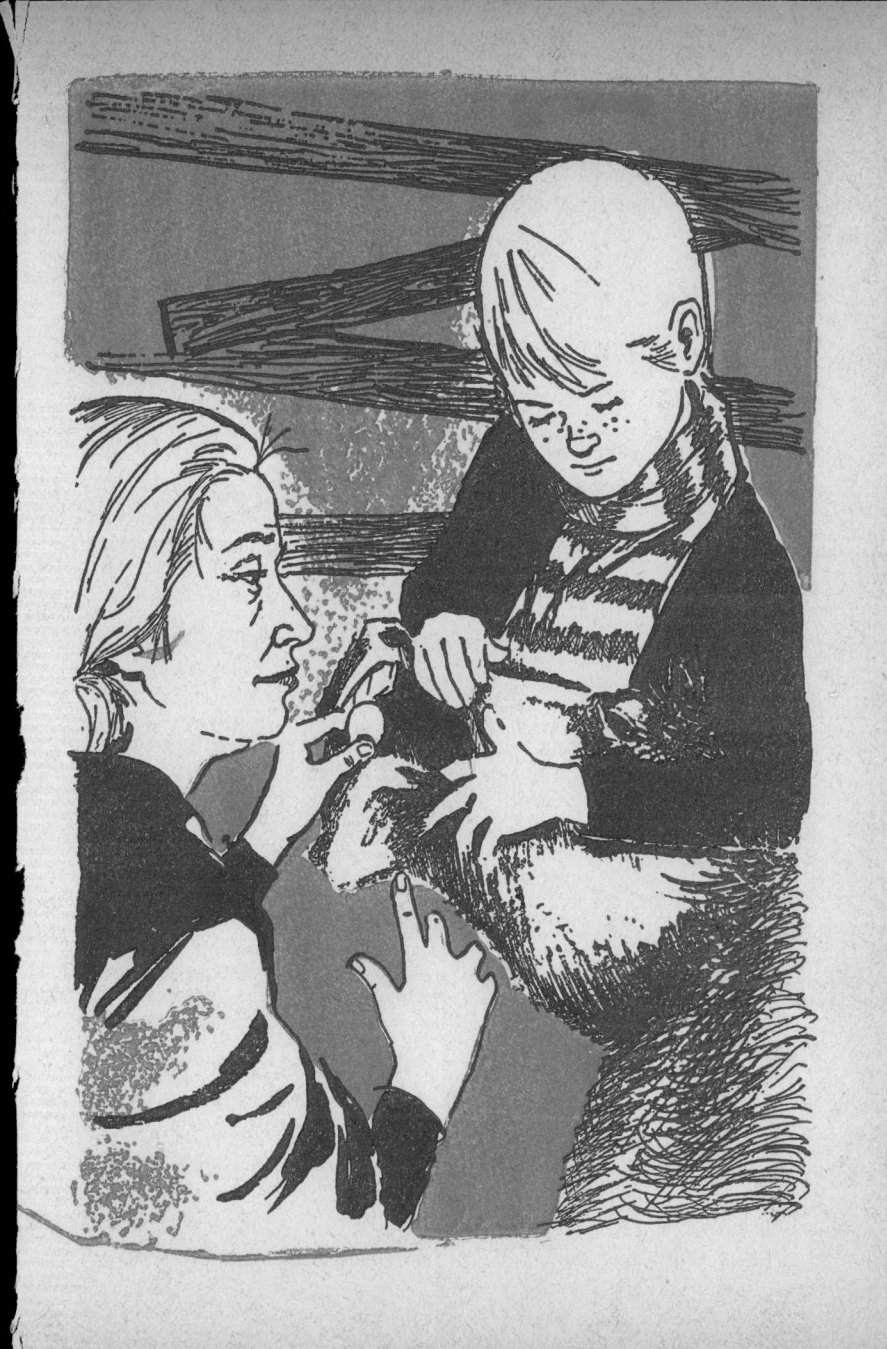

kettle of soup for supper was steaming away on the stove. Mrs. Wiggs did not believe in sacrificing present need to future comfort. She threw in a liberal portion of pepper, and, seizing the kettle in one hand and the bucket of tallow in the other, staggered back to the bonfire.

"Now, Billy," she commanded, "put this bucket of tallow down there in the hottest part of the fire. Look out! Don't tip it—there! Now, you come here an' help me pour this soup into the bottle. I'm goin' to git that ole hoss so het up he'll think he's havin' a sunstroke! Seems sorter bad to keep on pestering him when he's so near gone, but this here soup'll feel good when it once gits inside him."

When the kettle was empty the soup was impartially distributed over Mrs. Wiggs and the patient. But a goodly amount had "got inside," and already the horse was losing his rigidity.

Only once did Billy pause in his work and that was to ask, "Ma, what do you think I'd better name him?"

Giving names was one of Mrs. Wiggs's chief

accomplishments and usually required much thoughtful consideration. In this case, however, if there was to be a christening it must be at once.

"I'd like a jography name," suggested Billy, feeling that nothing was too good to bestow upon his treasure.

Mrs. Wiggs stood with the soup dripping from her hands and earnestly contemplated the horse. Babies, pigs, goats, and puppies had drawn largely on her supply of late, and geography names especially were scarce. Suddenly a thought struck her.

"I'll tell you what, Billy! We'll call him Cuby! It's a town I heared 'em talkin' 'bout at the grocery."

By this time the tallow was melted and Mrs. Wiggs carried it over by the horse. She put each of his hoofs into the hot liquid while Billy rubbed the legs with all the strength of his young arms.

"That's right," she said. "Now you run home an' git that piece of carpet by my bed an' we'll kiver him up. I'm goin' to git them fence rails over yonder to keep the fire goin'."

Through the long night they worked with their patient. And when the first glow of morning appeared in the east, a triumphant procession wended its way across the Cabbage Patch. First came an old woman bearing sundry pails, kettles, and bottles and next came a very sleepy little boy leading a trembling old horse, with soup all over its head, tallow on its feet, and a strip of rag carpet tied about its middle.

And thus Cuba, like his geographical namesake, emerged from the violent ordeal of reconstruction with a mangled constitution, internal dissension, a decided preponderance of foreign element, but a firm and abiding trust in the new power with which his fortunes had been irrevocably cast.

5

A Reminiscence

"It is easy enough to be pleasant
   When life flows along like a song,
But the man worth while is the one who will smile
   When everything goes dead wrong."

When Miss Hazy was awakened early that morning by a resonant neigh at the head of her bed, she mistook it for the trumpet of doom. Miss Hazy's cottage, as has been said, was built on the bias in the Wiggses' side yard, and the little lean-to, immediately behind Miss Hazy's bedroom, had been pressed into service as Cuba's temporary abode.

After her first agonized fright, the old woman ventured to push the door open a crack and peep out.

"Chris," she said in a tense whisper to her sleeping nephew, "Chris, what on airth is this here hitched to our shutter?"

Chris, usually deaf to all calls less emphatic than cold water and a broomstick, raised a rumpled head from the bedclothes.

"Where at?" he asked.

"Right here!" said Miss Hazy, still in a terrified whisper, and holding fast the door, as if the specter might attempt an entrance. Chris did not stop to adjust his wooden leg, but hopped over to the door and cautiously put an eye to the opening.

"Why, shucks, 'tain't nothin' but a hoss!" he said, in disgust, having nerved himself for nothing less than a rhinoceros, such as he had seen in the circus.

"How'd he git there?" demanded Miss Hazy.

Chris was not prepared to say.

All through breakfast Miss Hazy was in a flutter of excitement. She had once heard of a baby being left on a doorstep, but never a horse. When the limit of her curiosity was about reached, she saw Mrs. Wiggs coming across the yard carrying a bucket. She hastened to meet her.

"Mornin'," called Mrs. Wiggs brightly, in spite of her night's vigil. "Ain't we got a fine hoss?"

Miss Hazy put the ash barrel between herself and the animal and hazarded a timid inspection, while Mrs. Wiggs made explanations and called attention to Cuba's fine points.

"Can't you come in an' take a warm?" asked Miss Hazy, as she concluded.

"Well, I b'lieve I will," said Mrs. Wiggs. "I ain't been over fer quite a spell. The childern kin clean up, bein' it's Saturday." From seven to nine in the morning were the favorite calling hours in the Cabbage Patch.

Mrs. Wiggs chose the chair which had the least on it and leaned back smiling affably. She remarked, "We're used to hosses. This here's the second one we've had."

"My," said Miss Hazy, "you muster been well to do!"

"Yes," continued Mrs. Wiggs, "we was—up to the time of the fire. Did I ever tell you 'bout how Jim brought our other hoss to town?"

Miss Hazy had heard the story a number of

times, but she knew the duties of a hostess.

"It was this a-way," went on Mrs. Wiggs, drawing her chair closer to the fire and preparing for a good, long talk. "You see, me an' the childern was comin' on the steam-car train but ther' wasn't no way to git the hoss here, 'ceptin' fer somebody to ride him. Course Jim said he'd do it. Poor Jim, always ready to do the hard part!" She paused to wipe her eyes on her apron and Miss Hazy wept in sympathy.

"Never min', Miss Wiggs. Don't cry. Go on an' tell me what you done next."

"Well," said Mrs. Wiggs, swallowing the lump in her throat, "Jim said he'd go. He never had been to the city, an' he was jes' a little shaver, but I knowed I could trust him."

"I don't see how you could stand to risk it!" exclaimed Miss Hazy.

"Oh, I reckon whatever you *got* to do, you *kin* do. I didn' see no other way. So one mornin' I put a old patch quilt over the hoss, tied a bucket of oats on behin', an' fixed some vittles fer Jim, an' started 'em off. It was a forty-mile ride to the city, so I calkerlated to start Jim so's he'd git to Dr. White's 'bout nightfall."

"Dr. White was your old doctor, wasn't he?" prompted Miss Hazy.

"Yes'm, he used to 'tend Mr. Wiggs before we moved over into Bullitt County. You know Mr. Wiggs was a widow man when I married him. He had head trouble. Looked like all his inflictions gethered together in that head of hisn. He uster go into reg'lar transoms!"

Miss Hazy was awe-struck, but more dreadful revelations were to follow.

"I guess you knew I killed him," continued Mrs. Wiggs calmly. "The doctor an' ever'body said so. He was jes' gitten over typhoid, an' I give him pork an' beans. He was a wonderful man! Kept his senses plumb to the end. I remember his very las' words. I was settin' by him, waitin' fer the doctor to git there, an' I kep' sayin', 'Oh, Mr. Wiggs! You don't think you are dyin', do you?' an' he answered up jes' as natural an' fretful-like, 'Good lan', Nancy! How do I know? I ain't never died before.' An' them was the very las' words he ever spoke to anybody."

"Was he a church member, Miss Wiggs?" inquired Miss Hazy.

"Well, no, not exactly," admitted Mrs. Wiggs reluctantly. "But he was what you might say a well-wisher. But, as I was tellin' you, Dr. White was a old friend, an' I pinned a note on Jim's coat tellin' who he was an' where he was goin', an' I knowed the doctor would have a eye on him when he got as fur as Smithville. As fer the rest of the trip I wasn't so certain. The only person I knowed in the city was Pete Jenkins, an' if there was one man in the world I didn't have no use fer, it was Pete. But when I don't like folks I try to do somethin' nice fer 'em. Seems like that's the only way I kin weed out my meanness. So I jes' sez to Jim, 'You keep on astin' till you git to Number Six Injun House, an' then you ast fer Pete Jenkins. You tell him,' sez I, 'you are Hiram Wiggs's boy, an' as long as he done so much harm to yer pa, mebbe he'd be glad to do a good turn by you an' keep you an' the hoss fer the night, till yer ma comes fer you.' Well, Jim started off lookin' mighty little settin' up on that big hoss, an' I waved my apron long as I could. Then I hid behin' a tree to keep him from seein' me cry. He rode all that day an' 'bout sundown he come to Dr. White's. Pore little feller, he was so tired an' stiff he couldn't hardly walk, but he tied the hoss to the post an' went 'round to the back door an' knocked real easy. Mrs. White come to the door an' sez, real cross, 'No, doctor ain't here,' an' slammed it shut agin. I ain't meanin' to blame her. Mebbe her bread was in the oven, or her baby cryin', or somethin', but seems to me I couldn't have treated a dog that a-way!

"Pore Jim, he dragged out to the road agin, an' set there beside the hoss, not knowin' what to do nex'. Night was a-comin' on, he hadn't had no supper, an' he was dead beat. By an' by he went to sleep an' didn't know nothin' till somebody shuck his shoulder an' sez, 'Git up from here! What you doin' sleepin' here in the road?' Then he went stumblin' 'long, with somebody holdin' his arm, an' he was took into a big, bright room, an' the doctor was lookin' at him an' astin' him questions. An' Jim said he never did know what he answered but it must 'a' been right, fer the doctor grabbed holt of his hand an' sez, 'Bless my soul! It's little Jimmy Wiggs, all the way from Curryville!'

"Then they give him his supper, an' Mrs. White sez, 'Where'll he sleep at, Doctor? There ain't no spare bed.' Then Jim sez the doctor frowned like ever'thin' an' sez, 'Sleep? Why, he'll sleep in the bed with my boys. An' they orter be proud to have sech a plucky bedfeller!'

"Jim never did fergit them words. They meant a good deal more to him than his supper.

"Early the nex' mornin' he started out agin, the doctor pointin' him on the way. He didn't git into the city till 'long 'bout four o'clock, an' he sez he never was so mixed in all his life. All my childern was green about town. It made ever' one of 'em sick when they first rode on the streetcars. An' Europena was skeered to death of the newsboys 'cause she thought they called 'Babies,' 'stid of 'Papers.' Jim kep' right on the main road like he was tole to, but things kep' a-happenin' 'round him so fast, he said he couldn't do no more'n jes' keep out o' the way. All of a suddint a ice wagon come rattlin' up behin' him. It was runnin' off, an' 'fore he knowed it a man hit it in the head an' veered it 'round towards him. Jim said his hoss turned a clean somerset, an' he was th'owed up in the air, an'—"

"Ma!" called a shrill voice from the Wiggses' porch. "Australia's in the rain barrel!"

Mrs. Wiggs looked exasperated. "I never was havin' a good time in my life that one of my children didn't git in that rain barrel!"

"Well, go on an' finish," said Miss Hazy, to whom the story had lost nothing by repetition.

"Ther' ain't much more," said Mrs. Wiggs, picking up her bucket. "Our hoss had two legs an' his neck broke, but Jim never had a scratch. A policeman took him to Number Six Injun House an' Pete Jenkins jes' treated him like he'd been his own son. I was done cured then an' there fer my feelin' aginst Pete."

"Ma!" again came the warning cry across the back yard.

"All right, I'm comin'! Good-by, Miss Hazy. You have a eye to Cuby till we git our shed ready. He ain't as sperited as he looks."

And with a cordial hand shake Mrs. Wiggs went cheerfully away to administer chastisement to her erring offspring.

6

A Theater Party

"The play, the play's the thing!"

Billy's foreign policy proved most satisfactory, and after the annexation of Cuba many additional dimes found their way into the tin box on top of the wardrobe. But it took them all, besides Mrs. Wiggs's earnings, to keep the family from the awful calamity of "pulling agin a debt."

One cold December day Billy came in and found his mother leaning wearily on the table. Her face brightened as he entered, but he caught the tired look in her eyes.

"What's the matter?" he asked.

"Ain't nothin' the matter, Billy," she said, trying to speak cheerfully. "I'm jes' wore out, that's all. It'll be with me like it was with Uncle

Ned's ole ox, I reckon. He kep' a-goin' an' a-goin' till he died a-standin' up. An' even then they had to push him over."

She walked to the window and stood gazing absently across the commons. "Do you know, Billy," she said suddenly, "I've got the craziest notion in my head. I'd jes' give anythin' to see the show at the Opery House this week."

If she had expressed a wish for a diamond necklace Billy could not have been more amazed, and his countenance expressed his state of mind.

Mrs. Wiggs hastened to explain, "Course, I ain't really thinkin' 'bout goin' but them show bills started me to studyin' 'bout it an I got to wishin' me an' you could go."

"I don't 'spect it's much when you git inside," said Billy, trying negative consolation.

"Yes, 'tis, Billy Wiggs," answered his mother impressively. "You ain't never been inside a theayter, an' I have. I was there twict, an' it was grand! You orter see the lights, an' fixin's, an' all the fine ladies an' their beaux. First time I went they was a man in skin tights a-walkin' on a rope h'isted 'way up over ever'body's head."

"What's skin tights?" asked Billy, thrilled in spite of himself.

"It's spangles 'round yer waist an' shoes without no heels to 'em. You see, the man couldn't wear many clothes 'cause it would make him too heavy to stay up there in the air. The band plays all the time an' folks sing an' speechify, an' ever'body laughs an' has a good time. It's jes' grand, I tell you!"

Billy's brows were puckered and he sat unusually quiet for a while looking at his mother. Finally he said, "You might take my snow money from las' week."

Mrs. Wiggs was indignant. "Why, Billy Wiggs!" she exclaimed. "Do you think I'd take an' go to a show when Asia an' Australia ain't got a good shoe to their backs?"

Billy said no more about the theater. But that afternoon when he was out with the kindling he pondered the matter deeply. It was quite cold and sometimes he had to put the reins between his knees and shove his hands deep into his pockets to get the stiffness out of them. It really seemed as if everybody had just laid in a supply of kindling. The shadowy little plan he had been forming was growing more shadowy all the time.

"I 'spect the tickets cost a heap," he thought ruefully, as he drew himself up into a regular pretzel of a boy. "But then, she never does have no fun an' never gits a thing fer herself." And because Billy knew of his mother's many sacrifices, and because he found it very hard to take Jim's place, a lump lodged in his throat and gave him so much trouble that he forgot for a while how cold he was.

About this time he came within sight of the Opera House. Tantalizing posters appeared advertising the GREATEST EXTRAVAGANZA OF THE CENTURY. He pulled Cuba into a walk and sat there absorbing the wonders depicted. Among the marvels were crowds of children dressed as butterflies, beautiful ladies marching in a line, a man balancing a barrel on his feet, and—yes, there was the man in "skin tights" walking on the rope!

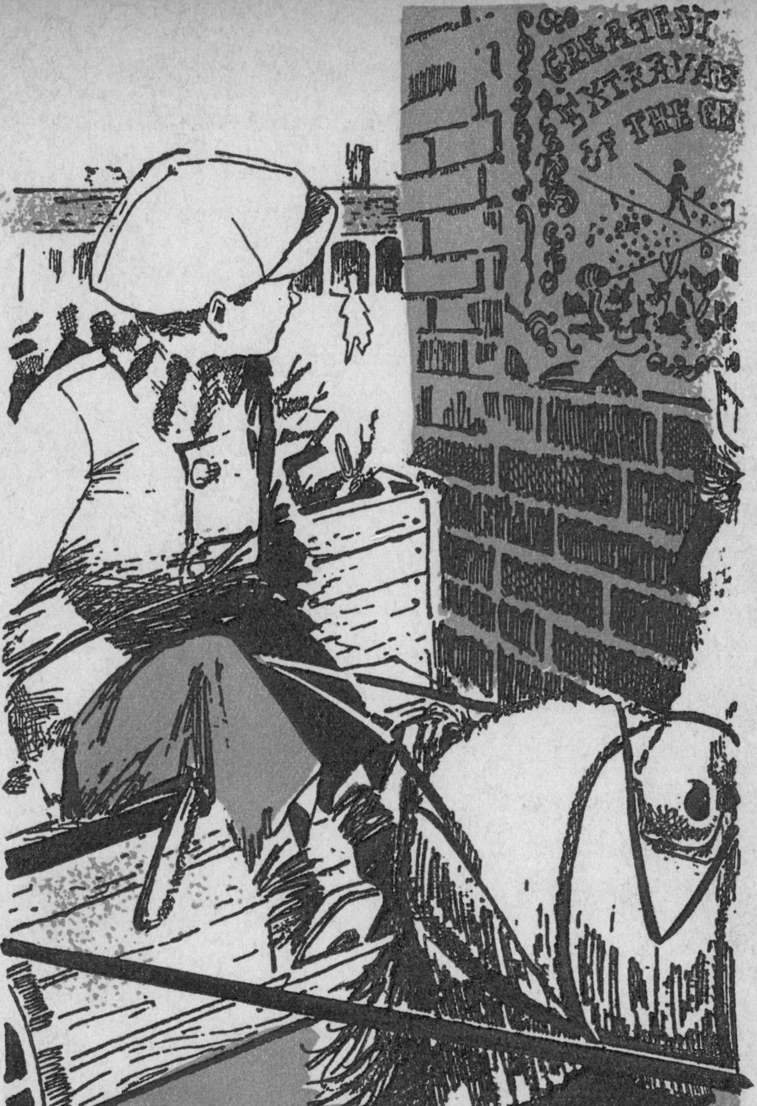
GREATEST
EXTRAVAG
OF THE CE

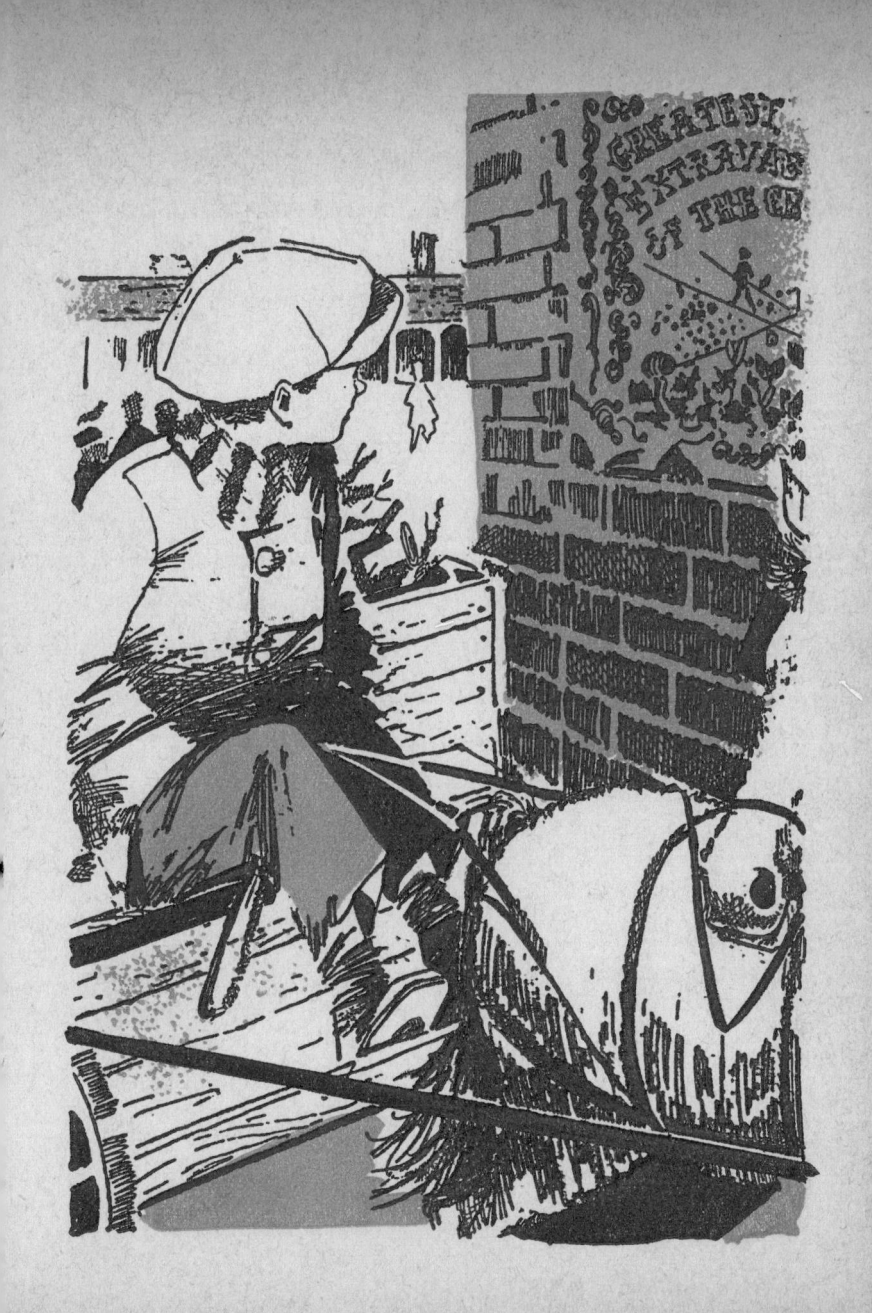

A keen puff of wind brought Billy back to his senses, and as his longing eyes turned from the gorgeous show bills they encountered the amused look of a gentleman who had just come out of the Opera House. He was so tall and fine-looking that Billy thought he must own the show.

"Some kindlin', sir?"

The gentleman shook his head. The posters still danced before Billy's eyes. If his mother could only see the show! The last chance seemed slipping away. Suddenly a bold idea presented itself. He got out of the wagon and came up on the step.

"Couldn't you use a whole load if I was to take it out in tickets?"

The man looked puzzled. "Take it out in tickets?" he repeated.

"Yes, sir," said Billy, "theayter tickets. Don't you own the show?"

The gentleman laughed. "Well, hardly," he said. "What do you want with more than one ticket?"

There was a certain sympathy in his voice,

in spite of the fact that he was still laughing, and before Billy knew it he had told him all about it.

"How many tickets could yer gimme fer the load?" he asked, in conclusion.

The gentleman made a hurried calculation. "You say you have three sisters?" he asked.

"Yep," said Billy.

"Well, I should say that load was worth about five tickets."

"Gee whiz!" cried the boy. "That 'ud take us all!"

He followed the gentleman back to the ticket office and eagerly watched the man behind the little window count out five tickets and put them in a pink envelope.

"One for you, one for your mother, and three for the kids," said his friend, as Billy buttoned the treasure in the inside pocket of his ragged coat.

He was so excited that he almost forgot his part of the bargain but as the gentleman was turning away he remembered.

"Say, mister, where must I take the kindlin' to?"

"Oh, that's all right. You can sell it tomorrow," answered the man.

Billy's face fell instantly. "If you don't take the kindlin', I'll have to give you back the tickets. Ma don't 'low us to take nothin' that way."

"But I don't need the kindling. I haven't any place to put it."

"Ain't you got no home?" asked Billy incredulously.

"No," answered the man shortly.

The idea of any one, in any walk of life, not having any use for kindling was a new one to Billy. But he had no time to dwell on it for this new complication demanded all his attention.

"Ain't there nobody you could give it to?" he asked.

The gentleman was growing impatient. "No, no, go along. That's all right."

But Billy knew it would not be all right when he got home, so he made one more effort. "How'd you like to send it out to Miss Hazy?" he inquired.

"Well, Miss Hazy, not having the pleasure of my acquaintance, might object to the delicate attention. Who is she?"

"She's Chris's aunt. They ain't had no fire fer two days."

"Oh!" said the man heartily. "Then take it to Miss Hazy, by all means. Tell her it's from Mr. Bob who is worse off than she is, for he hasn't even a home."

An hour later there was wild excitement under the only tin roof in the Cabbage Patch. Such scrubbing and brushing as was taking place!

"It's jes' like a peetrified air castle," said Mrs. Wiggs, as she pressed out Asia's best dress. "Here I been thinkin' 'bout it, an' wantin' to go, an' here I am actually gittin' ready to go! Come here, child, and let me iron out yer plaits while the iron's good an' hot."

This painful operation was performed only on state occasions. Each little Wiggs laid her head on the ironing board, a willing sacrifice on the altar of vanity, while Mrs. Wiggs carefully ironed out five plaits on each head. Europena was the only one who objected to being a burnt offering. But when she saw the frizzled locks of the others her pride conquered her fear, and, holding tight to Billy's hand, she bent her chubby head to the trying ordeal.

"Now, Billy, you run over to Mrs. Eichorn's an' ast her to loan me her black crepe veil. Mrs. Krasmier borrowed it yesterday to wear to her pa's funeral, but I guess she's sent it back by this time. An', Billy—Billy, wait a minute—you be sure to tell 'em we're goin' to the show." Mrs. Wiggs vigorously brushed her hair with the clothesbrush as she spoke. Australia had thrown the hairbrush down the cistern the summer before.

"Asia, you go git the alpaca from behind the chest an' sorter shake it out on the bed."

"Who's goin' to wear it, Ma?" The question came in anxious tones, for the blue alpaca had been sent them in a bundle of old clothes, and though it failed to fit either of the girls, the wearing of it was a much coveted privilege.

"Well, now, I don't know," said Mrs. Wiggs,

critically surveying the children. "It won't button good on you and it swags in the back on Australia."

"Lemme wear it, Ma!"

"No, lemme!" came in excited tones.

Mrs. Wiggs had seen trouble before over the blue alpaca. She knew what anguish her decision would bring to one or the other.

"It really looks best on Asia," she thought, "but if I let her wear it Austry'll have a cryin' spell an' git to holdin' her breath an' that'll take up too much time." So she added aloud, "I'll tell you what we'll do. Asia, you kin wear the skirt an' Austry kin wear the jacket."

But when she had pinned the skirt over one little girl's red calico dress and buttoned the blue jacket over the clean pinafore of the other, she looked at them dubiously. "They do look kinder mixed," she admitted to herself, "but I reckon it don't matter, so long as they're both happy."

Just then Billy came in with the veil in one hand and a bunch of faded carnations in the other hand.

"Look, Ma!" he exclaimed, holding up his trophy. "I swapped 'em with Pete fer a top an' a agate. He got 'em outen a ash barrel over on the avenue."

"Well, now, *ain't* that nice?" said Mrs. Wiggs. "I'll jes' clip the stems an' put 'em in a bottle of water. By the time we go they'll be picked up right smart. I wisht you had something to fix up in, Billy," she added. "You look as seedy's a rasbury."

Billy did look rather shabby. His elbows were out and two of the holes in his pants were patched and two were not. Mrs. Wiggs was rummaging in the table drawer.

"I wisht I could find somethin' of yer pa's that would do. Here's his white gloves he wore the time he was pallbearer to ol' Mr. Bender. Seems to me they do wear white gloves to the theayter, but I disremember."

"Naw! I ain't a-goin' to wear no gloves," said Billy firmly.

Mrs. Wiggs continued her search. "Here's yer grandpa's watch fob but I'm skeered fer you to wear it. You might lose it. It's a family remnant—been handed down two generations. What about this here red comforter? It would sorter spruce you up an' keep you warm, besides. You know you've had a cold fer a week an' yer pipes is all stopt up." So it was decided, and Billy wore the comforter.

At seven o'clock they were ready, and, the news having spread abroad that the Wiggses were going to a show, many of the neighbors came in to see how they looked and to hear how it happened.

"Some of you shake down the stove an' pull the door fer me. I am jes' that skeered of hurtin' Mrs. Eichorn's veil I'm 'fraid to turn my head," said Mrs. Wiggs nervously as she stepped off the porch.

The little procession had left the railroad tracks far behind when Mrs. Wiggs stopped suddenly.

"Fer the land's sakes alive! Do you know what we've gone an' done? We have left the theayter tickets to home!"

At this Australia began to cry and a gloom settled upon the party.

"Billy, you run back fast as yer legs kin carry you an' look in that tin can behind the clock. We'll wait right here fer you." Mrs. Wiggs wrapped Europena in her shawl and tried to keep up the spirits of the party as they huddled on the curbing to await Billy's return.

"Look how pretty it looks, all them lights a-streamin' out the winders on the snow. Looks like a chromo Ma used to have."

But the young Wiggses were in no frame of mind to appreciate the picturesqueness of the scene.

It was very cold and even the prospect of the show was dimmed by the present discomfort. By and by Australia's sobs began anew.

"What's the matter, honey? Don't cry. Billy'll be back in a little while an' then we'll git in where it's good an' warm."

"I want my supper!" wailed Australia.

Then it dawned on Mrs. Wiggs for the first time that, in the excitement of preparation, supper had been entirely overlooked.

"Well, if that don't beat all!" said she. "I had jes' 'bout as much idea of supper as a goat has of kid gloves!"

But when Billy came flying back with the tickets, and the party had started once more on the long walk to the Opera House, the enticing posters began to appear and supper and the cold were forgotten.

7

"Mr. Bob"

> "If his heart at high floods
> Swamped his brain now and then,
> 'Twas but richer for that
> When the tide ebbed again."

A large audience assembled that night to witness THE GREATEST EXTRAVAGANZA OF THE CENTURY. The Opera House was a blaze of light and color.

From the recesses of one of the boxes Redding made a careful survey of the faces beneath him. First nights usually found him there with the same restless, eager look in his eyes. Tonight he evidently failed to find what he sought and was turning listlessly away when he stopped suddenly, bent forward, then smiled broadly. He had caught sight of Billy's red comforter.

The boy's hair was plastered close to his head

and his face was transformed by soap and happiness. Redding glanced quizzically at the rest of the party—at the mother's radiant countenance beaming from the dusk of her crepe veil, at the three little girls in their composite costumes, at the carnations pinned on each bosom. Then he deliberately turned his back on THE GREATEST EXTRAVAGANZA OF THE CENTURY and centered his attention on the motley group.

It was a singularly enthusiastic theater party, oblivious of surroundings and lost in wonder at the strange sights. Billy's laugh rang out frequently with refreshing spontaneity. Their enjoyment was so evident that Redding was surprised at the close of the first act to see them put on their wraps and march solemnly out of the theater. He hastened to the lobby and touched Billy on the shoulder.

"Didn't you like the show?" he asked.

"You bet!" said Billy, his eyes shining and his cheeks flushed.

Mrs. Wiggs was hopelessly entangled in the crepe veil but her ideas of etiquette were rigid.

She disengaged one hand and said with dignity, "I 'low this is Mr. Bob, Billy's friend. Happy to meet yer acquaintance. Asia, speak to the gentleman—Australia—Europena!" with a commanding nod at each.

Three small hands were thrust at Redding simultaneously and he accommodated them all in his broad palm.

"But why are you going home?" he asked, looking from one to the other.

"Where else would we go to?" asked Mrs. Wiggs in amazement.

"Why not stay and see the play out? That was only the first act."

"Is there some more, Ma?" asked Asia eagerly.

"Why, of course," explained Redding, "lots more. Now, go back and stay until everybody has left the theater, and then you will be certain it's over."

So back they went, furnishing an amusing between acts diversion for the impatient audience.

After the curtain descended on the final scene,

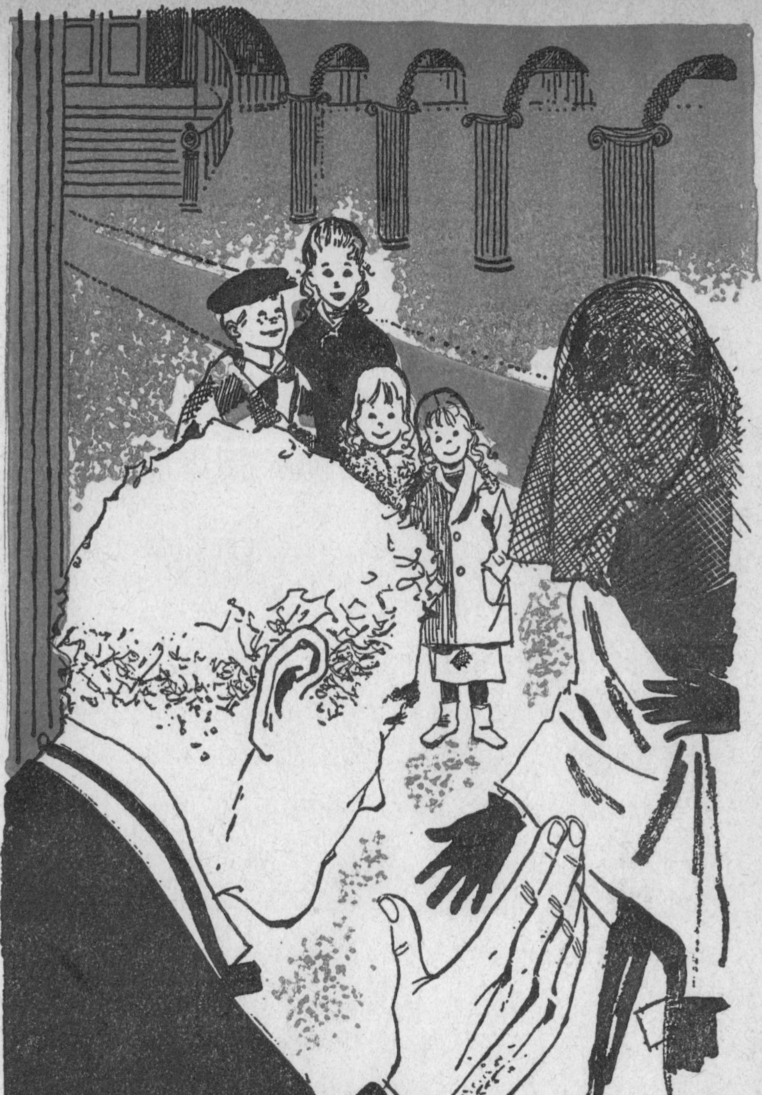

Redding waited in the lobby while the stream of people passed. The Wiggses had obeyed instructions and were the very last to come out. They seemed dazed by their recent glimpse into fairyland. Something in their thin bodies and pinched faces made Redding form a sudden resolve.

"Billy," he said gravely, "can't you and your family take supper with me?"

Billy and his mother exchanged doubtful glances. For the past three hours everything had been so strange and unbelievable that they were bewildered.

"You see, we will go right over to Bond's and have something to eat before you go home," urged Redding.

Mrs. Wiggs was in great doubt, but one of the little girls pulled her skirt and said in pleading tones, "Ma, let's do!" And Billy was already casting longing eyes at the big restaurant across the way. She had not the heart to refuse. As they were crossing the street Asia stopped suddenly and cried, "Ma, there's the 'Christmas Lady' gittin' in that cab! She seen us! Look!"

But before they could turn, the cab door had slammed.

Redding took them into a small apartment curtained off from the rest of the café so only the waiters commented on the strange party. At first there was oppressive silence. Then the host turned to Europena and asked her what she liked best to eat.

A moment of torture ensued for the small lady, during which she nearly twisted her thumb from its socket, then she managed to gasp, "Green pups!"

Mr. Bob laughed. "Why, you little cannibal!" he said. "What on earth does she mean?"

"Cream puffs," explained Mrs. Wiggs airily. "She et 'em onct at Mrs. Reed's, the Bourbon Stock Yard's wife, an' she's been talkin' 'bout 'em ever sinct."

After this the ice, while not broken, at least had a crack in it, and by the time the first course was served Redding was telling them a funny story and three of the audience were able to smile. It had pleased him to order an elaborate supper and he experienced the keenest enjoyment over the novelty of the situation. The Wiggses ate as he had never seen people eat before. "For speed and durability they break the record," was his mental comment. He sat by and, with consummate tact, made them forget everything but the good time they were having.

As the supper progressed Mrs. Wiggs became communicative. She still wore her black cotton gloves and gestured with a chicken croquette as she talked.

"Yes," she was saying, "Jim was one o' them handy childern. When he was eight years old he could peddle as good as you could! I guess you heard 'bout our roof. Ever'body was talkin' 'bout it. Billy is takin' right after him. Do you know what that boy has gone an' done? He's built his pa a monumint!"

"A monument!" exclaimed Redding.

"Yes, sir, a tombstun monumint! I was allers a-wishin' that Mr. Wiggs could have a monumint, and Billy never said a word but he set his head to it. One day he come home with a lot of these here tiles what they had throwed out from the tile fact'ry. Some of 'em was jes' a little nicked an' the others was jes' as good as new. Well, he kep' on gittin' 'em ever' day or two till he had a consider'ble pile. Ever' night he used to set on the floor an' fool with them things, a fittin' 'em here an' crackin' 'em off there, but I never paid no 'tention to him. One night, when I come in from Mrs. Eichorn's, what did I see on the floor but a sure-'nough tombstun slab. An' spelt out in little blue tiles down the middle was:

'Pa. Gone, but not forgotten.'

I was jes' that pleased I set down an' bust out cryin'. We made a sorter box to hold it, an' chinked it up with cement, an' las Sunday me an' the childern took it out an' fixed it up on Mr. Wiggs's grave. Some day we're goin' to make Jimmy one; you know Jimmy's my boy that's dead." Her eyes filled and her lips trembled. Even the sunshine of her buoyant nature could not dispel one shadow that always lay across her heart.

At this moment Billy, doubtless thrilled at being the topic of conversation, upset his glass of water, and the deluge descended full upon Australia, drenching the jacket of the blue alpaca. Such a wail as arose! Threats and persuasion were alike unavailing. She even refused to be mopped off, but slid in a disconsolate heap under the table. Redding attempted to invade the citadel with an orange as a flag of truce, but his overtures were ineffectual and he was compelled to retreat under fire.

"I'd leave her be, Mr. Bob," advised Mrs. Wiggs placidly, as she spread her salad on a piece of bread. "She'll git to holdin' her breath if you notice her."

The shrieks gradually diminished to spasmodic sobs which in turn gave place to ominous silence.

"Billy," said Redding, taking Mrs. Wiggs's advice and ignoring the flood sufferer, "how would you like to be my office boy?"

"I'd like it a heap," answered Billy promptly.

Redding turned to Mrs. Wiggs. "You see, it's a newspaper office, and while the pay isn't much at first, still it's better than peddling kindling, and there would be a chance for promotion as he got older."

"Oh, yes," answered Mrs. Wiggs complacently, "there wouldn't be no trouble 'bout Billy promotin'. I 'spect he could take to writin' newspapers right away if you could hold him down to it. He's jes' like his pa—the very spittin' image of him! Mr. Wiggs was so educated—the most fluent man in jography I ever seen!"

"I'm goin' to be like Mr. Bob when I grow up," said Billy stoutly. His recollection of his paternal parent was not the sort ideals are made of.

Just here the waiter appeared with the final course and Asia lifted the tablecloth and whispered, "Say, 'Straly, we've got ice cream." No answer. Then little Europena, with baby wisdom, put her towhead under the cloth and said, " 'Traly, it's pink!" and Australia emerged, tear-stained but smiling, and finished her supper on Mr. Bob's knee.

When the limit of capacity had been tested to the fullest and Billy had declared that "he couldn't swaller no more, he was jes' chawin'," Redding filled their pockets with candy and, when Mrs. Wiggs was not looking, put a quarter in each hand. Then he rang for a carriage, and in spite of Mrs. Wiggs's protestations he put them in and repeated Billy's directions as to the exact location of the Cabbage Patch.

"My, my, ain't this nice!" said Mrs. Wiggs, leaning back against carriage cushions for the first time in her life, while Redding lifted Europena in beside her.

"We've seed a good time fer onct in our lives," said Asia. It was the first time she had spoken since they left the theater.

"Lemme ride up on top, Ma!" demanded Billy, eagerly.

"Lemme, too, lemme!" came from the sleepy Australia who did not know what new attraction was being offered but was resolved not to miss anything.

"All right, Billy. But, Austry, you must stay with Ma. Good-by, Mr. Bob, and thanks—thanks fer one an' all!"

Redding stood on the corner where they had left him, and the smile died out of his face. Within a block was a jolly crowd and a hearty welcome; across the street was the big apartment house where his dark and cheerless window promised him nothing. For a moment he stood irresolute. "There is certainly nobody to care where I go," he thought gloomily; then suddenly the smile came back. "But if I'm to be Billy Wiggs's model I guess I'd better go to bed." He ran lightly across the street and up the broad stone steps.

8

Mrs. Wiggs At Home

*"She had a sunny nature that sought, like
a flower in a dark place, for the light."*

On Christmas day Lucy Olcott stood by the library window and idly scratched initials on the frosty pane. A table full of beautiful gifts stood near, and a great bunch of long-stemmed roses on the piano filled the room with fragrance. But Lucy evidently found something more congenial in the dreary view outside. She was deep in thought when the door opened and Aunt Chloe came in with a basket and a note.

The old woman grinned as she put the basket on the floor. "You might 'a' knowed it wuz fum dem Wiggses," she said.

Lucy opened the note and read:

> Dear miss Lucy the basket of cloths and vittles come. We or so mutch obliged, and asia wore the read dress to the soshul and enjoyed her selph so. Mutch I wish you could a went. Billy liked his hock and ladar and romcandons. Me and the childern want to send you a crismas mess of some of all we lade in for to live on. They is pertaters 2 kines, onions, termaters, a jar of vinegar and a jar perservs. I boughten the peeches last summer, they was gitting a little rotting so I got them cheep. Hope you will Enjoy them. I send some of all we got but Cole and Flower. Thankes thankes to you for your kind fealings.
>
> From yours no more
> MRS WIGGS.

"Bless her old heart!" cried Lucy. "That's the biggest widow's mite I ever saw. Put the basket there with my other presents, Aunt Chloe. It's worth them all."

She went over to the fire and held her hands to the friendly blaze. There was a restless, discontented look in her eyes that proved only too plainly that her Christmas was not a happy one.

"I wish it was night," she said. "I hate Christmas afternoon! Mother is asleep and it's too early for callers. I believe I'll go down to the Cabbage Patch."

Aunt Chloe stuck out her lip and rolled her eyes in deprecation.

"Don' you do it, honey. What you wanter be foolin' 'round wif dat po' white trash fer? Why don' you set heah by de fiah an' bleach yer han's fer de party tonight?"

"Bother the old party!" said Lucy impatiently.

Fifteen minutes later she was tramping through the snow, her cheeks glowing and her spirits rising. The Wiggses, while always interesting, had of late acquired a new significance. Since seeing them in the theater lobby with Robert Redding she had found it necessary to make several visits to the Cabbage Patch. The chief topic of conversation had been Mr. Bob: how he had taken them to the show; had made Billy his office boy; had sent them a barrel of apples and was coming to see them some day. To which deluge of information Lucy had listened with outward calmness and inward thrills.

Today as she entered the Wiggses' gate a shout greeted her. Billy let himself down from the chicken-coop roof and ran forward.

"Them Roman candles wasn't no good!" he cried. "One of 'em busted too soon and 'most blowed my hand off."

"Oh, no, it didn't, Miss Lucy!" said Mrs. Wiggs who had hastened out to meet her. "Them Roman candons was fine. Billy's hand wasn't so bad hurt he couldn't shoot his gum-bow shooter and break Miss Krasmier's winderpane. I'll be glad when tomorra comes an' he goes back to the office! Come right in," she continued. "Asia, dust off a cheer fer Miss Lucy. That's right. Now, lemme help you off with yer things."

"Lemme hold the muff!" cried Australia.

"No—me—me!" shrieked Europena.

A center rush ensued during which the muff was threatened with immediate annihilation. The umpire interfered.

"Australia Wiggs, you go set in the corner with yer face to the wall. Europena, come here!" She lifted the wailing little girl to her lap and looked her sternly in the eye. "If you don't hush this minute, I'll spank your doll!"

The awful threat was sufficient. Mrs. Wiggs had long ago discovered the most effectual way of punishing Europena.

When peace was restored Lucy looked about her. In each window was a piece of holly tied with a bit of red calico, and on the partly cleared table she saw the remains of a real Christmas dinner.

"We had a grand dinner today," said Mrs. Wiggs, following her glance. "Mr. Bob sent the turkey. We et all we wanted an' got 'nough left fer the rest of the week, countin' hash an' soup an' all. Asia says she's goin' to hide it, so as I can't

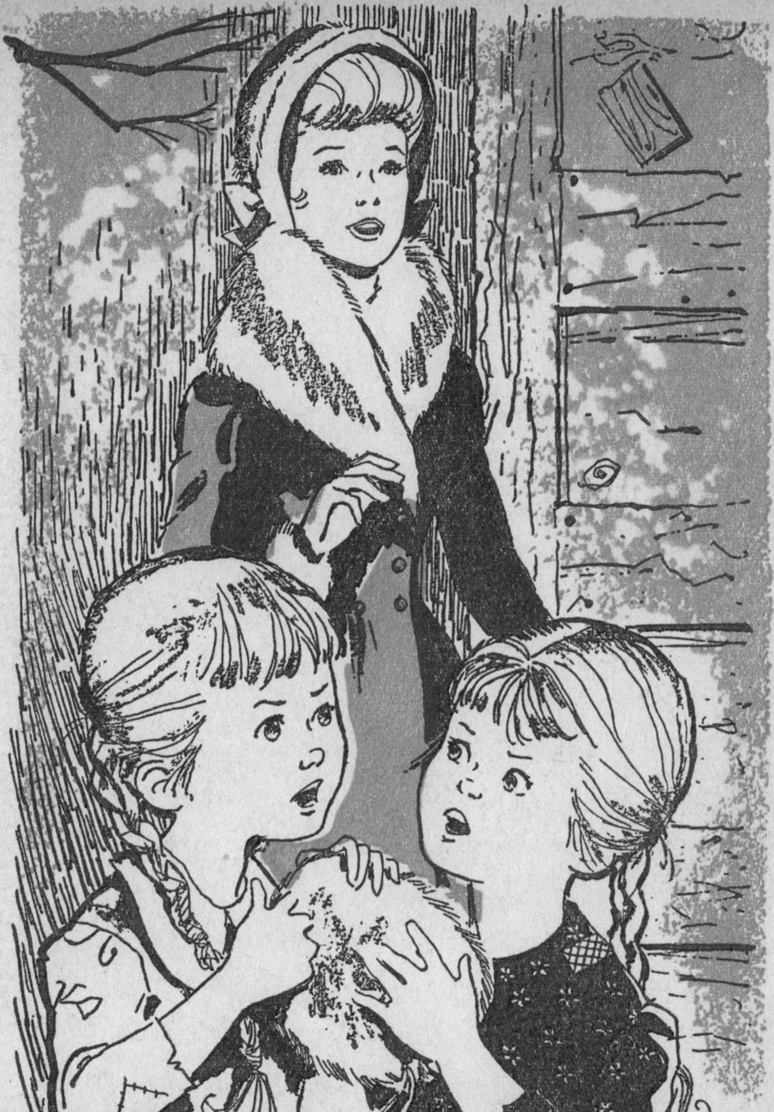

give no more away. By the way, do you notice what Asia's doin'?"

Lucy went to the window where Asia was busily working. This taciturn little girl, with her old, solemn face and clever fingers, was her favorite of the children.

"What are you making?" she asked, as the child dipped a brush into one of three cans which stood before her.

"She's paintin' a picture," announced Mrs. Wiggs proudly. "Looked like she was jes' crazy 'bout picture painting, an' I said, 'Well, Asia, if you have made up yer mind to be a artist, guess you'll have to be one.' Seems like when folks kin do pianner playin' an' picture paintin' it ain't right to let 'em wash dishes an' clean up all the time. So I went to a store an' ast fer some paint to make pictures with, and they wanted seventy cents fer a little box full. Ain't that a mighty heap, Miss Lucy, jes' fer plain paint, 'fore it's made up into flowers an' trees an' things? Well, anyway, I couldn't git it but I come home an' got me three tin cans an' took 'em 'round to Mr. Becker's paint shop. An' he poured me a little red an' yaller an' blue an' only charged me a nickel an' throwed in a brush. Asia's painted a heap with it. I'll show you some of her things."

It was not necessary, for in every direction Lucy looked her eyes were greeted with specimens of Asia's handiwork. Across the footboard of the bed was a spray of what might have passed for cauliflower. The tin boiler was encircled by a wreath of impressionistic roses, and on the windowpane a piece of exceedingly golden goldenrod bent in an obliging curve in order to cover the crack in the glass.

"It's perfectly wonderful!" said Lucy, with entire truthfulness.

"Ain't it?" said Mrs. Wiggs, with the awed tone one uses in the presence of genius. "Sometimes I jes' can't believe my eyes when I see what my childern kin do! They inherit their education after Mr. Wiggs. He was so smart an' b'longed to such a fine fambly. Why, Mr. Wiggs had real Injun blood in his veins. His grandpa was a squaw —a full-blood Injun squaw!"

Lucy made an heroic effort to keep a solemn face as she asked if Asia looked like him.

"Oh, my, no!" continued Mrs. Wiggs. "He was a blunette—real dark complected. I remember when he fus' come a-courtin' me folks thought he was Italian. Pa wasn't, to say, well off in them days." Mrs. Wiggs never applied superlatives to misfortunes. "He had a good many of us to take keer of, an' after Mr. Wiggs had been keepin' company with me fer 'bout two weeks he drove up one night with a load of coal an' kindlin' an' called Pa out to the fence. 'Mr. Smoot,' sez he, 'as long as I am courtin' your daughter I think I orter furnish the fire to do it by. Ef you don't mind,' sez he, 'I'll jes' put this wagonload of fuel in the coal house. I 'spect by the time it's used up Nance'll be of my way of thinkin'.' An' I was!" added Mrs. Wiggs, laughing.

Ordinarily Lucy found endless diversion in listening to the family reminiscences but today another subject was on her mind.

"How is Billy getting along?" she asked.

"Jes' fine!" answered Mrs. Wiggs. "Only he

comes home at night 'most dead. I give him money to ride, but ever' day last week he et up his nickel."

"Who—who has charge of him now?" Lucy blushed at her subterfuge.

"Mr. Bob," said Mrs. Wiggs. "He's the gentleman that took us to supper. He's got money. Asia said he give the waiter a quarter. Billy is jes' crazy 'bout Mr. Bob. Says he's goin' to be jes' like him when he grows up. He will, too, if he sets his head to it! Only he never kin have them big brown eyes an' white teeth Mr. Bob's got. Why, when Mr. Bob smiles it jes' sort of breaks up his whole face."

Lucy's eyes were fixed on the mammoth butterfly upon whose iridescent wings Asia was putting the finishing touches but her thoughts were far away.

"I jes' wish you could see him!" went on Mrs. Wiggs enthusiastically.

"I wish I could!" said Lucy, with such fervor that Mrs. Wiggs paused on her way to answer a knock at the outside door.

There was a scraping of feet in the passage.

"I have been driving all over the country looking for you," said a man's voice. "I have some Christmas presents for the kids."

Lucy rose hastily and turned just as Redding entered.

"Mr. Bob, this is Miss Lucy," announced Mrs. Wiggs triumphantly. "She was jes' 'lowin' she'd like to see you."

If a blue-eyed angel straight from the peaks of paradise had been presented to him, Redding could not have been more astounded nor more enraptured.

But to Lucy it was a moment of intense chagrin and embarrassment. During the long silence of the past year she had persuaded herself that Redding no longer cared for her. To be thrust upon him in this way was intolerable. All the blood in her veins rushed to her face.

"Do you know where my muff is, Mrs. Wiggs?" she asked, after a formal greeting.

"Oh! You ain't a-goin'?" asked the hostess, anxiously. "I wanted you all to git acquainted."

"Yes, I must go," said Lucy hurriedly, "if you will find my muff."

She stood nervously pulling on her gloves while Mrs. Wiggs searched for the lost property. There was a deafening tumult in her heart, and though she bit her lips to keep from laughing, the tears stood in her eyes.

"Austry's under the bed," announced Europena, who had joined in the quest.

"I ain't!" came in shrill, indignant tones as Mrs. Wiggs dragged forth the culprit and restored the muff.

"May I drive you over to the avenue? I am going that way." It was Redding's voice, but it sounded queer and unnatural.

"Oh, no! No, thank you," gasped Lucy, hardly knowing what she said. Her one idea was to get away before she broke down completely.

Redding held the door open as she passed out. His face was cold, calm, inscrutable; not a quiver of the mouth, not a flutter of the lids, but the light went out of his eyes and hope died in his heart.

Mrs. Wiggs stood watching the scene in perplexity.

"I dunno what ailed Miss Lucy," she said, apologetically. "Hope it wasn't the toothache."

9

How Spring Came to the Cabbage Patch

"The roads, the woods, the heavens, the hills
  Are not a world today—
But just a place God made for us
  In which to play."

When the last snow had melted and the water was no longer frozen about the corner pump, the commons lost their hard, brown look and a soft green tinge appeared instead. There were not many ways of telling when spring came to the Cabbage Patch. No trees shook forth their glad little leaves of welcome, no anemones and snowdrops brought the gentle message. Even the birds that winged their way from the southland hurried by without so much as a chirp of greeting.

But the Cabbage Patch knew it was spring, nevertheless; something whispered it in the air. A dozen little signs gave the secret away; weeds were springing up in the fence corners, the puddles which a few months ago were covered with ice now reflected bits of blue sky, and the best token of all was the bright, warm sunshine that clung to the earth as if to love it back into beauty and life again.

One afternoon Mrs. Wiggs stood at her gate talking to Redding. It was the first time he had been there since Christmas day, for his first visit had been too painful for him to desire to repeat it.

"Yes, indeed, Billy kin go," Mrs. Wiggs was saying. "I'm mighty glad you drove him by home to git on his good coat. He never was to the fair grounds before. It'll be a big treat. How's Mr. Dick today?"

"No better," said Redding. "He coughed all night."

"He was takin' a nap o' sleep when I went to clean up this mornin'," said Mrs. Wiggs, "so I didn't disturb him. He ain't fer long, pore feller!"

"No, poor chap," said Redding sadly.

Mrs. Wiggs saw the shadow on his face and hastened to change the subject. "What do you think of Asia's fence?" she asked.

"What about it?"

"She done it herself," said Mrs. Wiggs. "That an' the pavement, too. Mrs. Krasmier's goat et up her flowers las' year, an' this year she 'lowed she'd fix it different. Chris Hazy, that boy over yonder with the peg stick, helped her dig the post-holes but she done the rest herself."

"Well, she is pretty clever!" said Redding, almost incredulously, as he examined the fence and sidewalk. "How old is she?"

"Fourteen, goin' on fifteen. Asia, come here."

The girl left the flower bed she was digging and came forward.

"Not a very big girl, are you?" said Redding, smiling at her. "How would you like to go up to the tile factory and learn to do decorating?"

Her serious face lit up with great enthusiasm. She forgot her shyness and said eagerly, "Oh, yes, sir! Could I?"

Before Redding could answer, Mrs. Wiggs broke in, "You'd be gittin' a artist, Mr. Bob! Them fingers of hers kin do anything. Last fall she built that there little greenhouse out of ol' planks an' kep' it full of flowers all winter. Put a lamp in durin' the cold spell. You orter see the things she's painted. And talk about mud pictures! She could jes' take some of that there mud under that hoss's feet an' make it look so much like you, you wouldn't know which was which."

Billy's appearance at this moment saved Redding from immediate disgrace.

"You come to the office with Billy in the morning," he called to Asia as they started off. "We'll see what can be done."

Asia went back to her digging with a will. The prospect of work, of learning how to do things right, and, above all, of learning how to paint, filled her with happiness.

"If I was you I'd make that bed in the shape of a star," said her mother, breaking in on her reflections. "Why don't you make it a mason star? Yer pa was a fine mason; it would be a sort of compliment to him."

"What is a mason star like?" asked Asia.

"Well, now I ain't right sure whether it's got

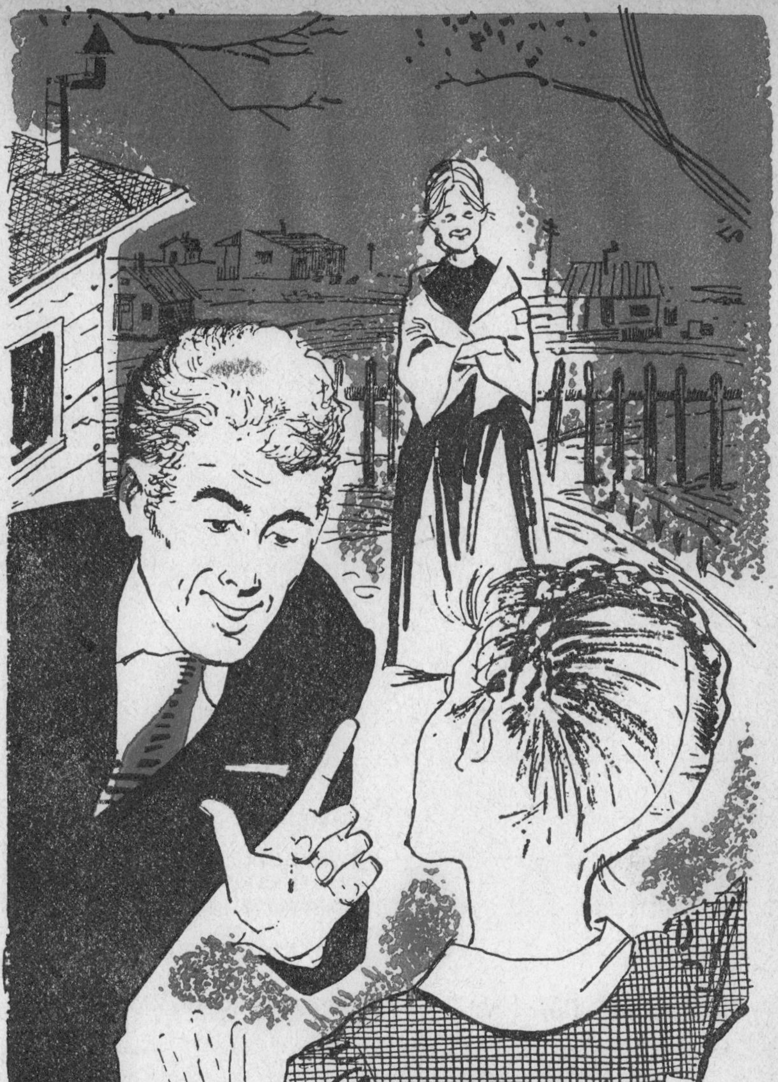

five points or six. Either way will do. Lands alive, I do believe there comes Miss Lucy!"

Lucy Olcott had been a frequent visitor of late. Through Mrs. Wiggs she had gotten interested in Mrs. Schultz and often stopped in to read to the bedridden old lady. Here, of course, she heard a great deal about the Eichorns, the elite of the Cabbage Patch, whose domestic infelicities furnished the chief interest in Mrs. Schultz's life. Lucy had even stood on a chair, at the invalid's earnest request, to count the jars of preserves in the Eichorn pantry. Later she had become acquainted with Miss Hazy, the patient little woman in monochrome, whose whole pitiful existence was an apology when it might have been a protest.

In fact, Lucy became an important personage in the neighborhood. She was sought for advice, called upon for comfort, and asked to share many joys. Her approach was usually heralded by a shout, "That's her a-comin'!" and she was invariably escorted across the commons by a guard of ragged but devoted youngsters. And the friendship of these simple people opened her eyes to the great problems of humanity. As she worked among them and knew life as it was, the hard little bud of her girlhood blossomed into the great soft rose of womanhood.

"Didn't you meet Mr. Bob up the street?" asked Mrs. Wiggs, as she led the way into the kitchen. "Him an' Billy have jes' left, goin' out to the fair grounds. Mr. Bob's jes' naturally the best man I ever set eyes on, Miss Lucy! Got the biggest heart, an' always doin' something kind fer folks. Jes' now talkin' 'bout gittin' Asia a place at the tile fact'ry. I don't see how you missed 'em! If he'd a sawn you with them vi'lets in yer belt, an' them roses in yer cheeks, I bet he wouldn't 'a' went."

"Oh, yes, he would!" said Lucy emphatically. "My roses don't appeal to Mr. Bob."

"Well, he likes yer eyes, anyway," said Mrs. Wiggs, determined to carry her point.

"Who said so?" demanded Lucy.

"He did. I ast him. I said they was regular star-eyes, jes' shining blue with them black eyelashes rayin' out all 'round, an' he said yes, that was the right name fer 'em—star-eyes."

There was a mist over the star-eyes as Lucy turned away.

"That's right, set right down there by the winder. It's so pretty out today it makes you feel good clean down yer back."

"I believe you always feel that way," said Lucy, pulling off her gloves. "Don't you ever worry over things?"

Mrs. Wiggs grew serious. "I'm lonesome fer Jimmy all the time," she said simply. "Some folks goes right under when trouble comes, but I carry mine fur an' easy."

"I don't mean grieving," said Lucy. "I mean worrying and fretting."

"Well, yes," admitted Mrs. Wiggs, taking a hot iron from the stove, "I've done that, too. I remember onct last winter I was tooken sick an' got to pesterin' 'bout what the children 'ud do if I died. They wasn't no money in the house an' they didn't know where to git none. All one night I laid there with my head 'most bustin' jes' worryin' 'bout it. By an' by I was so miserable I ast the Lord what I mus' do an' he tole me." There was absolute conviction in her tone and manner. "Nex' mornin'," she went on, "soon's I could I went over to the 'spensary an' ast fer the chief doctor.

" 'Doctor,' I sez, 'don't you buy corpses?'

" 'Yes,' sez he, lookin' kinder funny.

" 'Well,' sez I, 'I want to sell mine.'

"Then I tole him all 'bout it an' ast him if he wouldn't take my body after I was gone an' give the money to the childern.

" 'Will you put it in writin'?' sez he.

" 'Yes,' sez I, 'if you'll do the same.'

"So he drawed up the papers an' we both signed. An' a man with a spine in his back an' a lady with the rheumatiz witnessed it. So you see," concluded Mrs. Wiggs, "I didn't die. You mark my words, it ain't never no use puttin' up yer umbrell' till it rains!"

Lucy laughed. "Well, you certainly practice what you preach."

"Not always," said Mrs. Wiggs. "I'm 'feared I

use' to worry some over Mr. Wiggs. T'words the last he uster pretty often—" Here Mrs. Wiggs tipped an imaginary bottle to her lips and gave Lucy a significant wink. Even in the strictest confidence she could not bear to speak of the weakness of the late lamented.

"But no matter how bad he done, he always tried to do better. Mr. Dick sorter puts me in mind of him 'bout that."

"Who is Mr. Dick?"

"He's Mr. Bob's friend. Stays at his rooms sence he was took down."

"Is Mr. Redding sick?" asked Lucy, the color suddenly leaving her face.

"No, it's Mr. Dick. He's consumpted. I clean up his room ever' mornin'. He coughs all the time, jes' like Mr. Wiggs done. Other day he had a orful spell while I was there. I wanted to git him some whisky but he shuck his head. 'I'm on the water cart,' sez he. 'Bob's drivin' it.' He ain't no fatter 'n a knittin' needle an' weaker 'n water. You orter see him watch fer Mr. Bob! He sets by the winder, all propped up with pillars, an' never tecks his eyes offen that corner. An' when Mr. Bob comes in an' sets down by him an' tells him what's goin' on, an' sorter fools with him a spell, looks like he picks up right off. He ain't got no folks nor nothin'—jes' Mr. Bob. He shorely does set store by him —jes' shows it ever' way. That's right, too. I hold that it's wrong to keep ever'thing bottled up inside you. Yer feelin's is like rasbury vinegar. If you're skeered to use 'em an' keep on savin' 'em, first thing you know they've done 'vaporated!"

Lucy's experience had proved the contrary, but she smiled bravely back at Mrs. Wiggs, with a new tenderness in her face.

"You have taught me lots cf things!" she said impulsively. "You are one of the best and happiest women I know."

"Well, I guess I ain't the best by a long sight but I may be the happiest. An' I got cause to be: four of the smartest childern that ever lived, a nice house, fair to middlin' health when I ain't got the rheumatiz, and folks always goin' clean out of the way to be good to me! Ain't that 'nough to make a person happy? I'll be fifty years old on the Fourth of July, but I hold there ain't no use in dyin' 'fore yer time. Lots of folks is walkin' 'round jes' as dead as they'll ever be. I believe in gittin' as much good outen life as you kin—not that I ever set out to look fer happiness—seems like the folks that does that never finds it. I jes' do the best I kin where the good Lord put me at, an' it looks like I got a happy feelin' in me 'most all the time."

Lucy sat silent for a while, gazing out of the window. Mrs. Wiggs's philosophy was having its effect. Presently she rose and untied the bundle she held.

"Here is a dress I brought for Asia," she said, shaking out the folds of a soft crepe.

"Umph, umph! Ain't that grand?" exclaimed Mrs. Wiggs, coming from behind the ironing board to examine it. "It does seem lucky that your leavin's jes' fits Asia, an' Asia's jes' fits Austry. There ain't no symptoms of them bein' handed down, neither! We all model right after you but it looks like Asia's the only one that ketches yer style. Oh, must you go?" she added, as Lucy picked up her gloves.

"Yes, I promised Mrs. Schultz to read to her this afternoon."

"Well, stop in on yer way back—I'll have a little present ready fer you." It was an unwritten law that no guest should depart without a gift of some kind. Sometimes it was one of Asia's paintings, again it was a package of sunflower seed, or a bottle of vinegar, and once Lucy had taken home four gourds and a bunch of paper roses.

"I declare, I never will git no work done if this weather keeps up!" said Mrs. Wiggs, as she held the gate open. "If I wasn't so stove up an' nobody wasn't lookin', I'd jes' skitter 'round this here yard like a colt!"

10

Australia's Mishap

" 'Tis one thing to be tempted,
Another thing to fall."

Through the long afternoon Mrs. Wiggs sang over her ironing and Asia worked diligently in her flower bed. Around the corner of the shed which served as Cuba's dwelling place, Australia and Europena made mud pies. Peace and harmony reigned in this shabby Garden of Eden until temptation entered and the weakest fell.

" 'Tain't no fun jes' keepin' on makin' mud pies," announced Australia, after enough pastry had been manufactured to start a miniature bakery.

"Wish we could make some white cakes like they have at Mr. Bagby's," said Europena.

"Could if we had some whitewash. I'll tell you what's let do! Let's take some of Asia's paint she's goin' to paint the fence with an' make 'em green on top."

"Ma wouldn't like it," protested Europena. "Besides, I don't want my little pies green."

"I'm goin' to," said Australia, beginning her search for the paint can. "It won't take but a little teeny bit. They'll never miss it."

After some time the desired object was discovered on a shelf in the shed. Its high position enhanced its value, giving it the cruel fascination of the unattainable.

"Could you stand up on my soldiers, like the man at the show?" demanded Australia.

"I'd fall off," said Europena.

" 'Fraid-cat!" taunted her sister, in disgust. "Do you reckon you could hol' the chair while I climbed up on the back?"

"It ain't got no bottom."

"Well, it don't need to have no bottom if I'm goin' to stand on its back," said Australia sharply. Leaders of great enterprises must of necessity turn deaf ears to words of discouragement.

"You might git killed," persisted Europena.

"'Twouldn't matter," said Australia loftily. "'Twouldn't be but the seventh time. I got three more times to die. 'Fore you was borned I was drownded out in the country, that was one time. Then I fell in the ash bar'l and was dead, that's two times. An'—an' then I et the stove polish, that's four times. An' I can't 'member, but the nex' time will be seven. I don't keer how much I git killed till it's eight times. Then I'm goin' to be good all the time 'cause when you are dead nine times they put you in a hole an' throw dirt on you!"

Australia had become so absorbed in her theory of reincarnation that she had forgotten the paint, but the bottomless chair recalled it.

"Now, you lay 'crost the chair, Europena, an' I'll climb up," she commanded.

Europena, though violently opposed to the undertaking, would not forsake her leader at a critical moment. She had uttered her protest, had tried in vain to stem the current of events;

nothing was left her now but to do or die. She valiantly braced her small body across the frame of the chair and Australia began her perilous ascent.

Cuba looked mildly astonished as the plump figure of the little girl appeared above his feed-box.

"I've 'most got it!" cried Australia, reaching as high as possible and getting her forefinger over the edge of the big can.

At this juncture Cuba, whose nose had doubtless been tickled by Australia's apron string, gave a prodigious sneeze. Europena, feeling that retribution was upon them, fled in terror. The ballast being removed from the chair, the result was inevitable. A crash, a heterogeneous combination of small girl, green paint, and shattered chair, then a series of shrieks that resembled the whistles on New Year's Eve!

Redding was the first to the rescue. He had just driven Billy to the gate when the screams began, and with a bound he was out of the buggy and rushing to the scene of disaster. The picture that met his eyes staggered him. Australia, screaming wildly, lay in what appeared to his excited vision to be a pool of green blood. Europena was jumping up and down beside her, calling wildly for her mother, while Cuba, with ears erect and a green liquid trickling down his nose, sternly surveyed the wreck. In a moment Redding had Australia in his arms and was mopping the paint from her face and hair.

"There, there, little sister, you aren't much hurt!" he was saying, as Mrs. Wiggs and Asia rushed in.

The damage done proved external rather than internal, so after assuring herself that no bones were broken Mrs. Wiggs constituted herself a salvage corps.

"Take off yer coat out here, Mr. Bob, an' I'll take off Austry's dress. Them's the worst, 'ceptin' her plaits. Now, we'll all go up to the kitchen, an' see what kin be did."

Now, Fate, or it may have been the buggy at the gate, decreed that just as they turned the corner of the house Lucy Olcott should be coming

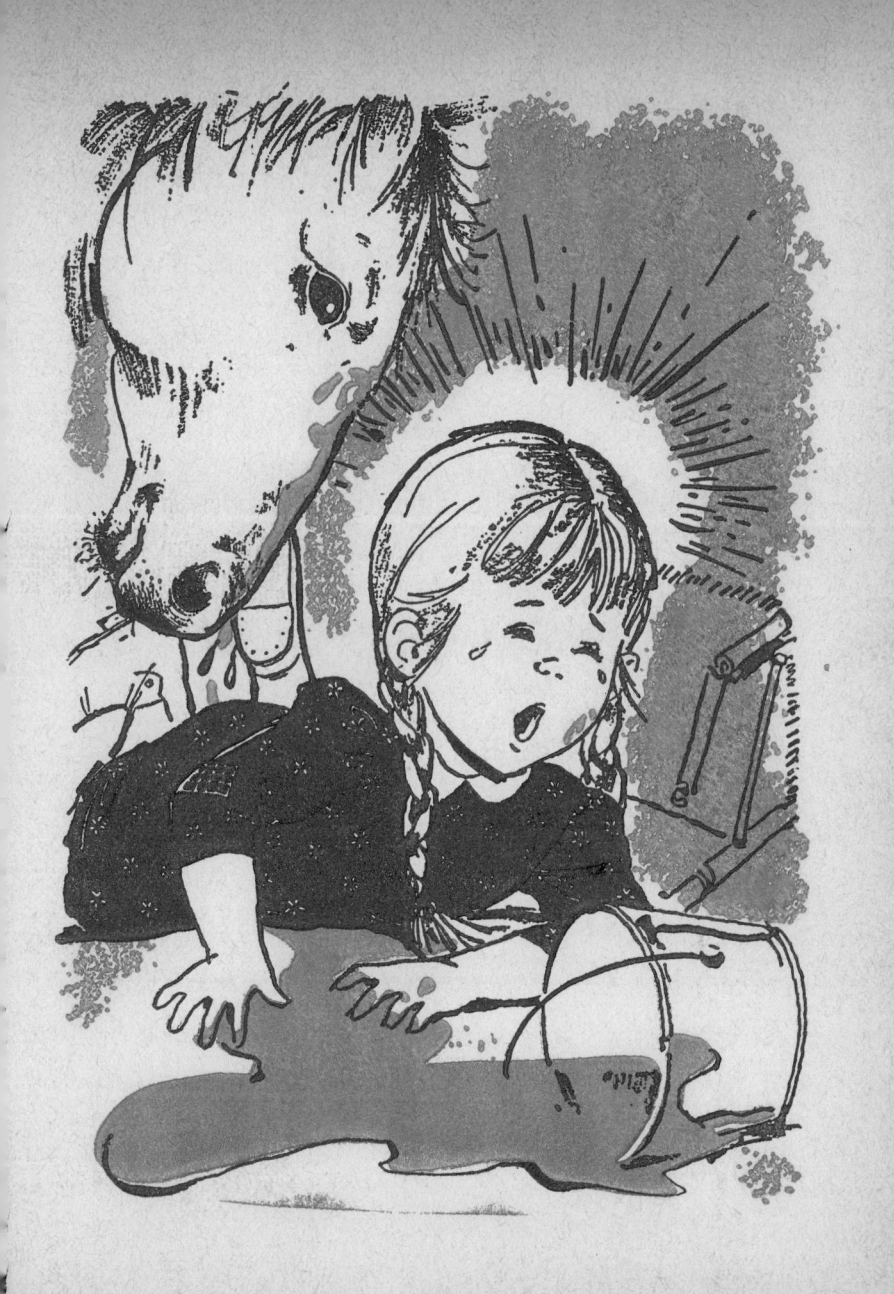

up the walk. For a moment she stood bewildered at the sight that greeted her. Redding, in his shirt sleeves, was leading Australia by the hand. The little girl wore a red flannel petticoat, and over her face and hands and to the full length of her flaxen braids ran sticky streams of bright green paint.

Involuntarily, Lucy looked at Redding for explanation and they both laughed.

"Ain't it lucky it was the back of her head 'stid of the front?" said Mrs. Wiggs, coming up. "It might 'a' put her eyes out. Pore chile, she looks like a Mollygraw! Come right in, an' let's git to work."

Billy was dispatched for turpentine. Lucy, with an apron pinned about her, began operations on Australia's hair, while Redding sat helplessly by, waiting for Mrs. Wiggs to make his coat presentable.

"I am afraid her hair will have to be cut," said Lucy ruefully, as she held up a tangled snarl of yellow and green.

"All right," Mrs. Wiggs said promptly. "Whatever you say is all right."

But Australia felt differently. Her sobs, suppressed for a time, broke forth afresh.

"I ain't goin' to have my hair cut off!" she wept. "Jes' leave it on this a-way."

Mrs. Wiggs commanded and Lucy entreated in vain. Finally Redding drew his chair up in front of the small girl.

"Australia, listen to me just a moment, won't you? Please!"

She uncovered one eye.

"You wouldn't want green hair, would you?"

A violent shake of the head.

"Well, if you will let Miss Olcott cut off all that ugly green hair and give the pretty curls a chance to grow back, I'll give you—let's see, what shall I give you?"

"A doll buggy an' dishes," suggested Europena, who was standing by.

"Yes," he said, "a doll buggy, and dishes, and a dollar besides!"

Such munificence was not to be withstood. Australia suffered herself to be shorn, in view of the future tempering of the wind.

"You orter been a hoss trainer, Mr. Bob," said Mrs. Wiggs admiringly, when the deed was accomplished. "Yer voice jes' makes folks do things!"

"Not everybody, Mrs. Wiggs," he said grimly.

"Where do you suppose Billy's went with the turkentine? I declare that boy would be a good one to send after trouble! Oh, you ain't goin' to try an' wear it this a-way?" she said, as Redding insisted on putting on his coat.

As he turned to the door a light hand touched his arm. Lucy unfastened the violets at her belt and timidly held them toward him.

"Will you take them—to Dick?" she faltered.

He looked at her in amazement. For a moment neither spoke, but her eyes made the silence eloquent. They told the secret that her lips dared not utter. There are times when explanations are superfluous. Redding threw discretion to the winds and, regardless of Wiggses and the consequences, took the "Christmas Lady" in his arms and kissed away the year of grief and separation.

It was not until Mrs. Wiggs saw their buggy disappear in the twilight that she recovered her speech.

"Well, it certainly do beat me!" she exclaimed, after a fruitless effort to reconstruct her standard of propriety. "I've heard of 'painters' colic,' but I never knowed it to go to the head before!"

11

The Benefit Dance

"Those there are whose hearts have a slope
southward, and are open to the whole
noon of Nature."

Notwithstanding the fact that calamities seldom come singly, it was not until the Fourth of July that the Cabbage Patch was again the scene of an accident.

Mrs. Wiggs had been hanging out clothes and was turning to pick up the empty basket, when Billy precipitated himself into the yard, yelling wildly.

"Chris Hazy's broke his leg!"

Mrs. Wiggs threw up her hands in horror. "Good lands, Billy! Where's he at?"

"They're bringin' him up the railroad track."

Mrs. Wiggs rushed into the house. "Don't let

on to Miss Hazy till we git him in," she cautioned, snatching up a bundle of rags and a bottle of liniment. "Pore chile! How it must hurt him! I'll run down the track an' meet 'em."

She was breathless and trembling from excitement as she turned the corner at Mrs. Schultz's. A crowd of boys were coming up the track, trundling a wheelbarrow, in which sat Chris Hazy, the merriest of the lot, waving a piece of his wooden leg in the air.

Mrs. Wiggs turned upon Billy.

"I never lied, Ma! I said he broke his leg," the boy gasped out as best he could for laughing, "an' you never ast which one. Oh, boys! Git on to the rags an' arniky!"

Such a shout went up that Mrs. Wiggs laughed with the rest, but only for a moment, for she spied Miss Hazy tottering toward them and she hastened forward to relieve her anxiety.

"It's his peg stick!" she shouted. "P-e-g stick!"

This information, instead of bringing relief to Miss Hazy, caused a fresh burst of tears. She sat down on the track, with her apron over her face and swayed backward and forward.

"Don't make much difference which one 'twas," she sobbed. "It would be 'bout as easy to git another sure-'nough leg as to git a new wooden one. That las' one cost seven dollars. I jes' sewed an' saved an' scrimped to git it, an' now it's—busted!"

The boys stood around in silent sympathy, and when nobody was looking Chris wiped his eyes on his coat sleeve. Miss Hazy's arrival had changed their point of view.

Mrs. Wiggs rose to the occasion.

"Boys," she said, and her voice had an inspiring ring, "I'll tell you what let's do! Let's give a benefit dance tonight an' buy Chris Hazy a new peg stick. Every feller that's willin' to help, hol' up his hand."

A dozen grimy hands were waved on high and offers of assistance came from all sides. Mrs. Wiggs saw that now was the time to utilize their enthusiasm.

"I'll go right back to the house an' git Asia to write out the tickets, an' all you boys kin sell ten apiece. Miss Hazy, you kin come over an' help me git the house ready, an' we'll put Chris to cleanin' lamp chimbleys."

Under this able generalship the work was soon under way. The boys were dispatched with the tickets and the house was being put straight—at least the parlor was. It would have required many days to restore order to the chaos that habitually existed in the house of Wiggs.

"Asia, you help me roll these here barrels out on the porch an' I'll mop up the floor," said Mrs. Wiggs. "Miss Hazy, you look 'round in the kitchen an' see if you can't find a taller candle. Seems like I put one in the sugar bowl—that's it! Now, if you'll jes' cut it up right fine it'll be all ready to put on the floor when I git done."

When the floor was dry and the candle sprinkled over it, Australia and Europena were detailed to slide over it until it became slick.

"Would you ast ever'body to bring a cheer, or would you have 'em already here?" asked Mrs. Wiggs.

"Oh, le's bring 'em ourselves!" insisted Asia,

who had been to a church social.

So a raid was made on the neighborhood, and every available chair borrowed and arranged against the parlor wall.

By noon the boys reported most of the tickets sold, and Mrs. Wiggs received the funds which amounted to six dollars.

It being a holiday everybody was glad to come to the dance, especially as the proceeds were to help little Miss Hazy.

At one time there threatened to be trouble about the music. Some wanted Uncle Tom, the old Negro who usually fiddled at the dances, but others preferred to patronize home talent and have Jake Schultz, whose accordion could be heard at all hours in the Cabbage Patch.

Mrs. Wiggs effected a compromise. "They kin take turn about," she argued. "When one gits tired the other kin pick up right where he left off, an' the young folks kin shake the'r feet till they shoes drop off. Uncle Tom an' Jake, too, is a heap sight better than them mud-gutter bands that play 'round the streets."

"Wisht we could fix the yard up some," said Asia, when there was nothing more to be done in the parlor.

"I got a Japanee lantern," suggested Miss Hazy doubtfully.

"The very thing!" said Mrs. Wiggs. "We'll hang it in the front door. Billy's makin' a jack-o'-lantern to set on the fence. Fer the land's sake! What's John Bagby a bringin' in here?"

The grocery boy, staggering under the weight of an ice-cream freezer and carrying something wrapped in white paper, came up the path.

"It's fer you," he said, grinning broadly. John was cross-eyed, so Miss Hazy thought he looked at Mrs. Wiggs, and Mrs. Wiggs was sure he was looking at Miss Hazy.

However, the card on the freezer dispelled all doubt:

> Fer mrs Wiggs on her 50 Birthday
> compelments of The Naybors.

Under the white paper was a large, white iced cake with a **W** in cinnamon drops on top.

"How'd they ever know it was my birthday?" exclaimed Mrs. Wiggs, in delight. "Why, I'd even forgot it myself! We'll have the cake fer the party tonight. Somehow, I never feel like good things b'long to me till I pass 'em on to somebody else."

This necessitated a supply of saucers and spoons, and friends were again called upon to provide as many as possible.

The Wiggses were quite busy until seven o'clock when they stopped to get dressed for the party.

"Where's Europena?" asked Asia.

Nobody had seen her for some time. A search was made and she was discovered standing on a chair in a corner of the parlor, calmly eating the cinnamon drops off the birthday cake. Fingers and mouth were crimson, and the first stroke of the W was missing. Billy was so indignant that he insisted on immediate punishment.

"No, I ain't a-goin' to whip her on my birthday, Billy. She's sorry. She says she is. Besides, the cake ain't spoiled. It's jes' a 'N' now, 'stid of a

'W,' an' N stands fer Nancy jes' as good as W stands fer Wiggs!"

The first guest to arrive was Mr. Krasmier. He had paid ten cents toward the refreshments and proposed to get his money's worth. Mrs. Eichorn came early, too, but for a different reason: She was very stout and her happiness for the evening depended largely upon the size of the chair she secured.

Half the spectators had arrived before the hostess appeared. Her delay was caused by the loss of her false curls, which she had not worn since the memorable night at the Opera House. They were very black and very frizzled and had been bought at a reduced price from a traveling salesman some ten years before. Mrs. Wiggs considered them absolutely necessary to her toilet on state occasions. Hence consternation prevailed when they could not be found. Drawers were upset and boxes emptied, but with no success.

When hope was about abandoned, Asia suddenly darted out to the shed where the children kept their playthings. When she returned she triumphantly displayed a battered doll, armless and footless, with a magnificent crowning glory of black, frizzled hair.

Mrs. Wiggs waited until all the guests assembled before she made her speech of thanks for the cake and ice cream. It was a very fine speech, having been written out beforehand by Mr. Bagby. It began, "Ladies and gents, it gives me pleasure—" but before Mrs. Wiggs got half through she forgot it and had to tell them in her own way how grateful she was. In conclusion she said, "Couldn't nobody be more obliged than what I am! Looks like nice things is always comin' my way. Hope God'll bless you all! The musicianers have come, so we'll begin the party with a Virginer reel."

The young people scampered to their places, and when Mr. Eichorn made a bow to Mrs. Wiggs she laughingly took her place at the head of the line. And at the first strains of "Old Dan Tucker" she went down the middle with a grace and spirit that flatly contradicted the little red fifty on the birthday cake.

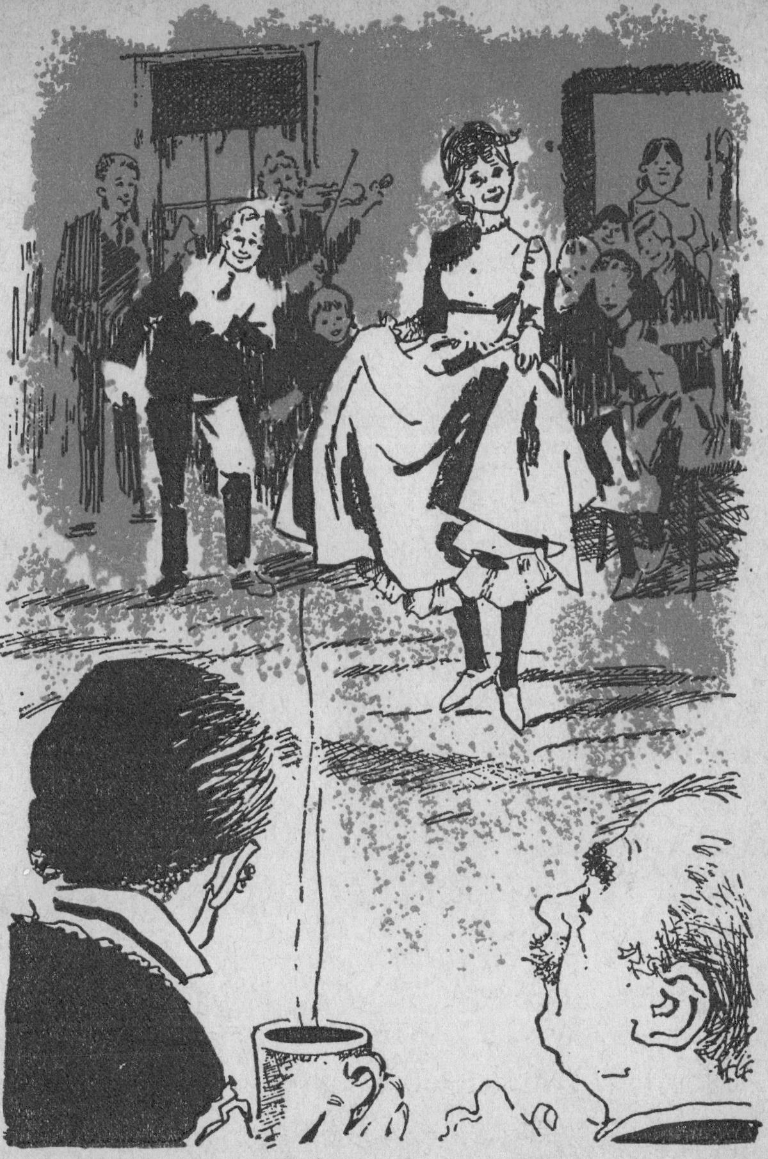

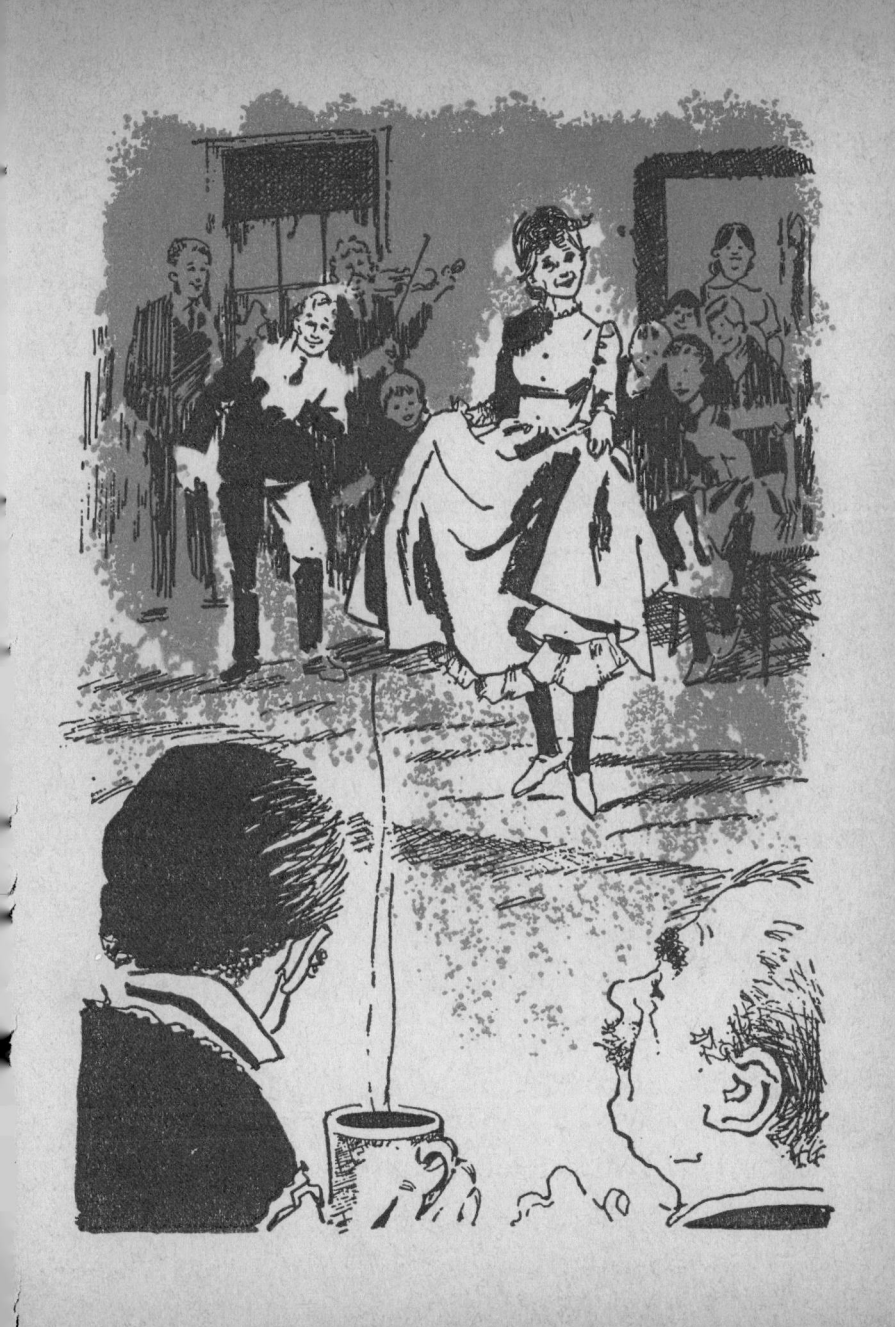

"Swing yer pahtners, balance all,
Swing dat gal wid a waterfall.
Skip light, ladies, de cake's all dough,
Nebber min' de weather,
so de win' don't blow."

Old Uncle Tom was warming up to his work, and the fun waxed furious. Asia, looking very pretty in her new crepe, cast shy glances at Joe Eichorn who had been "keeping company" of late. Billy, for whom there was no room in the reel, let off his energy in the corner by a noisy execution of the "Mobile Buck." Australia and Europena sat in the window with Chris Hazy and delightedly clapped time to the music.

When the dance ended, Mrs. Wiggs went to the door to get cool. She was completely out of breath, and her false curls had worked their way down over her eyebrows.

"Look—comin', Ma!" called Billy.

When Mrs. Wiggs saw who it was she hastened down to the gate.

"Howdy, Mr. Bob. Howdy, Miss Lucy! Can't you git right out an' come in? We're havin' a birthday party an' a benefit dance fer Chris Hazy's leg."

"No, thanks," said Redding, trying in vain not to look at Mrs. Wiggs's head. "We just stopped by to tell you the good news."

"'Bout Asia's position?" asked Mrs. Wiggs eagerly.

"Yes, about that and something else besides. What would you say if I told you that I was going to marry the prettiest, sweetest, dearest girl in the world?"

"Why, that's Miss Lucy!" gasped Mrs. Wiggs, more breathless than ever. Then the truth flashed upon her, and she laughed with them.

"Oh, sure 'nough! Sure 'nough! I'm jes' pleased to death!" She did not have to tell them. Her eyes, though suffering a partial eclipse, fairly beamed with joy and satisfaction. "An' so," she added, "it wasn't the paint, after all!"

When they had driven away, she lingered a moment at the gate. Music and laughter came from the house behind her as she stood smiling out across the moonlit Cabbage Patch. Her face still held the reflected happiness of the departed lovers, as the sky holds the rose tints after the sun has gone.

"An' they're goin' to git married," she whispered softly to herself. "An' Billy's got promoted, an' Asia's got a place, an' Chris'll have a new peg stick. Looks like ever'thin' in the world comes right, if we jes' wait long enough!"

Whitman CLASSICS

- Five Little Peppers Midway
- Freckles
- Wild Animals I Have Known
- Rebecca of Sunnybrook Farm
- Alice in Wonderland
- Mrs. Wiggs of the Cabbage Patch
- Fifty Famous Fairy Tales
- Rose in Bloom
- Eight Cousins
- Little Women

- Little Men
- Five Little Peppers and How They Grew
- Robinson Crusoe
- Treasure Island
- Heidi
- The Call of the Wild
- Tom Sawyer
- Beautiful Joe
- Adventures of Sherlock Holmes

Here are some of the best-loved stories of all time. Delightful... intriguing... never-to-be-forgotten tales that you will read again and again. Start your own home library of WHITMAN CLASSICS so that you'll always have exciting books at your finger tips.

Whitman
REG. U.S. PAT. OFF.

Whitman ADVENTURE and MYSTERY Books

Adventure Stories for GIRLS and BOYS...

TIMBER TRAIL RIDERS
  The Long Trail North
  The Texas Tenderfoot
  The Luck of Black Diamond

THE BOBBSEY TWINS
  In the Country
  Merry Days Indoors and Out
  At the Seashore

DONNA PARKER
  In Hollywood
  At Cherrydale
  Special Agent
  On Her Own
  A Spring to Remember
  Mystery at Arawak

TROY NESBIT SERIES
  The Forest Fire Mystery
  The Jinx of Payrock Canyon
  Sand Dune Pony

New Stories About Your Television Favorites...

Dr. Kildare
  Assigned to Trouble

Janet Lennon
  And the Angels
  Adventure at Two Rivers
  Camp Calamity

Walt Disney's Annette
  The Mystery at Smugglers' Cove
  The Desert Inn Mystery
  Sierra Summer
  The Mystery at Moonstone Bay

The Lennon Sisters
  Secret of Holiday Island

Leave It to Beaver

Ripcord

The Beverly Hillbillies

Lassie
  The Mystery at Blackberry Bog

Lucy
  The Madcap Mystery